Willing
to Believe

Among Other Books by the Author

Willing to Believe

The Controversy over Free Will

R. C. Sproul

Baker Books

A Division of Baker Book House Co
Grand Rapids, Michigan 49516

Published by Baker Books
a division of Baker Book House Company
P.O. Box 6287, Grand Rapids, MI 49516-6287

Second printing, January 1998

Printed in the United States of America

Library of Congress Cataloging-in-Publication Data

Sproul, R. C. (Robert Charles), 1939–
  Willing to believe : the controversy over free will / R. C. Sproul.
    p.   cm.
  Includes bibliographical references and index.
  ISBN 0-8010-1152-3
  1. Free will and determinism—Religious aspects—Christianity—History of doctrines. 2. Sin, Original—History of doctrines. 3. Grace (Theology)—History of doctrines. I. Title.
BT810.2.S694   1997
233'.7—dc21   97-18314

Portrait of Martin Luther (p. 86) painted by Lucas Cranach the Elder in 1528. Engraving of James Arminius (p. 124) by Thomas from a scarce Dutch print. Engraving of Jonathan Edwards (p. 146) from a portrait probably painted in 1751 by Joseph Badger. Photograph of Charles Grandison Finney (p. 168) taken by A. C. Platt of Oberlin.

For information about academic books, resources for Christian leaders, and all new releases available from Baker Book House, visit our web site:
http://www.bakerbooks.com

For information about Ligonier Ministries and the teaching ministry of R. C. Sproul, visit Ligonier's web site:
http://www.gospelcom.net/ligonier

To
Dr. James Montgomery Boice
Scholar, Pastor, Christian Leader
For his courageous ministry in the service of Christ
and his tireless efforts in the advancement of the
doctrines of grace.

Contents

Preface

*I*n the spring of 1996, a conference was held in Cambridge, Massachusetts, near the campus of Harvard University. The conference was hosted by the Alliance of Confessing Evangelicals for the purpose of calling the evangelical church to reaffirm its historic confessions. Special attention was given to the reaffirmation of the *sola's, sola fide, soli Christo, soli Deo gloria,* and *sola gratia.*

This present volume focuses on the issue of *sola gratia,* the underlying foundation of the issues that provoked the Reformation. It is an overview of the historical developments that grew out of the original controversy between Pelagius and Augustine. The stress is on the graciousness of grace and the monergistic work of God in effecting the believer's liberation from the moral bondage of sin. It explores the relationship between original sin and human free will.

Special thanks are in order to Maureen Buchman and Tricia Elmquist for their assistance in preparing the manuscript; to Ron Kilpatrick, librarian of Knox Theological Seminary, for his bibliographical assistance; and to Allan Fisher, my editor at Baker Book House.

R. C. Sproul
Orlando
Advent 1996

Illustrations and Figures

Illustrations

Figures

*H*ere was the crucial issue:
whether *God* is the author,
not merely of justification,
but also of faith. . . .

J. I. Packer and O. R. Johnston

Introduction

Evangelicalism and an Ancient Heresy

Perhaps the most ignominious event in the history of the Jewish nation prior to the destruction of Jerusalem in A.D. 70 was the Babylonian captivity. In 586 B.C. the Southern Kingdom was conquered by Nebuchadnezzar, and the Jewish elite were carried off to Babylon. There the people of God were faced with the onerous task of singing the Lord's song in a strange and foreign land. They were forced to hang their harps in the trees by the river Euphrates.

The Babylonian captivity was a time of testing, a crucible that produced spiritual giants such as Daniel and Ezekiel, and heroic champions of faith such as Shadrach, Meshach, and Abed-Nego. The flames of the crucible were made hot by the systematic pressure imposed on the Jewish people to adopt the ways of the pagan nation that held them hostage. Many of the interns undoubtedly capitulated and scrambled to assimilate their new environment.

There was a price to be paid for nonconformity; a severe cost for resistance to government and cultural mandates to acquiesce in the customs of paganism. It was an historical setting conducive to the practice of what Friedrich Nietzsche would later call a "herd morality."

Adjusting to the customs and worldview of one's environment is one of the strongest pressures people experience. To be "out of it" culturally is often considered the nadir of social achievement. People tend to seek acceptance and popularity in the forum of public opinion. The applause of men is the siren call, the Lorilee of paganism. Few are they who display the moral courage required for fidelity to God when it is unpopular or even dangerous to march to his drumbeat.

We remember Joseph, who was treacherously sold into foreign captivity and spent his younger years in a prison cell, but who nevertheless remained faithful to the God of his fathers, to the God of Abraham, Isaac, and Jacob. In Egypt Joseph was a congregation of one. Without the support of church or national custom, he resolved to be faithful to a God no one around him believed in except those converted by his testimony.

Our Babylonian Captivity

We do not live in Babylon. We enjoy a large measure of religious freedom and a cultural heritage that to a greater or lesser degree was built on the foundation of Christian faith. Yet the culture becomes increasingly hostile to biblical Christianity, and our faith is deemed more and more irrelevant to modern society. Ours has been described as the "post-Christian era," in which churches are likened to museums and biblical faith is regarded as an anachronism.

The cultural "Babylon" of our day is often described by evangelical Christians as the worldview espoused by so-called secular humanism. The rubric has been used as a magic word or phrase to capture all that is wrong with our culture. To be sure, secular humanism has a real face, but this worldview is but one of many systems competing with Christianity for the minds and souls of people.

The *secular* of secular humanism refers specifically to a worldview by which people understand the meaning and significance of human life. The term *secular* derives from the Latin *saeculum,* one of the Latin words for "world." In ancient Latin the two terms most frequently used to describe this world are *saeculum* and *mundus.* We derive the English word *mundane* from the latter. In the ancient world *mundus* usually referred to the world's spatial dimension, pointing specifically to the geographical "here" of our dwelling place. The term *saeculum* generally referred to the temporal mode of our existence, the "now" of our present life. Together the terms related to the "here and now" of this world.

On the surface it is not wrong or irreligious to speak of the here and now of human existence. Our lives are indeed lived out within the geographical confines of this planet, and we all measure our days by units of time that are at least subeternal. The problem is not with the word *secular.* The problem emerges when the three-letter suffix *ism* is attached to the otherwise docile word *secular.* The suffix indicates not so much a time frame as a philosophical worldview, a system by which life is understood and explained.

When the term *secular* is changed to *secularism,* the result is a worldview that declares that the now is all there is to human experience. It assumes that human experience is cut off from the eternal and the transcendent. We are told to grab all the gusto we can because "we only go around once." If God does exist, then in this view we have no access to him. We are marooned on alien soil where appeals to moral and philosophical absolutes are judged out of bounds. Ours is a time of existential crisis where meaning and significance are to be found in the realm of personal preference. We have truths, but no truth; purposes, but no purpose; customs, but no norms.

In the phrase *secular humanism* the word *secular* serves as an adjectival qualifier. It defines a particular strand of humanism. Humanism in various forms has been around for centuries. Some point to the pre-Socratic philosopher Protagoras as the original founder of this philosophy. His motto *homo mensura* defines the essence of humanism. It means that man is the measure of all things, that mankind represents the apex of living beings. There is nothing higher, no supreme being who reigns and rules over the affairs of human beings. In this case there is no ultimate distinction between a supreme being and a human being because the human being is the supreme being.

Though Protagoras is normally credited with founding ancient humanism, we can find its roots much earlier. This worldview was first presented as a philosophical option in the Garden of Eden. The irony is that it was introduced, not by a man, but by a snake. His motto was not *homo mensura,* but *sicut erat dei.* This Latin phrase translates the seductive promise of Satan to our primordial parents: "You shall be as gods" (Gen. 3:5).

The conflict between Christianity and secular humanism is a conflict about ultimates. This conflict allows no room for compromise. If God is ultimate, then manifestly man is not. Conversely if man is ultimate, then God cannot be. There can be only one ultimate. Compromise may be achieved in the realm of culture by tolerating competing worldviews. A secular nation may choose to "tolerate" Christianity to some degree as long as it is viewed merely as an expression of one form of human religion. But it cannot tolerate Christianity's truth claims. Christianity is always in a posture of antithesis with respect to secular humanism.

This antithesis makes it difficult for the modern Christian to maintain the integrity of faith in an alien culture. He must face the difficult choice of playing his harp or hanging it on the nearest tree. The Christian must be willing to be a pilgrim, a sojourner in a foreign land, if he expects to be faithful to Christ.

Perhaps the greatest threat to Israel was not the military might of foreign and hostile nations, but the dual threats of the false prophet within her gates and the constant temptation of syncretism. The two obviously went together. The favorite ploy of the false prophet was to obscure the antithesis between the ways of Yahweh and the practices of paganism. From the earliest days of conquest, Israel's history was one of syncretism, by which pagan thought and custom were assimilated by the covenant community. It was compromise with idolatry that destroyed Israel. Babylon was but the rod of punishment God wielded in chastising his people. Judgment fell on them (as canonical prophets like Jeremiah and Isaiah had forecast) precisely because the Jewish people mixed the impurities of paganism with the faith delivered to them by God.

The people of God have always had to live in antithesis. Every generation has been forced to face the seductive powers of syncretism. Church history is replete with examples of pagan ideas intruding into the church's mainstream. As strong a defender of biblical Christianity as Aurelius Augustine was, one may still find in his work traces of neo-Platonic thought and Manichaeism. This is ironic because the great theologian repudiated both pagan systems and devoted much time to combatting their theories. Greek concepts of immortality have crept into classical theology. Modern theology has been influenced by post-Kantian categories of thought, and some contemporary theologians have consciously attempted to synthesize Christianity and Marxism or Christianity and existentialism.

Robert Godfrey, president of Westminster Theological Seminary in Escondido, California, recently suggested that I write a book about "the myth of influence." I was startled by the suggestion because I did not know what he meant. He explained that this phrase refers to the modern evangelical penchant to "build bridges" to secular thought or to groups within the larger church that espouse defective theologies.

The mythical element is the naive assumption that one can build bridges that move in one direction only. Bridges are usually built to allow traffic to move in two directions. What often happens when we relate to others is that we become the influencees rather than the influencers. In an effort to win people to Christ and be "winsome," we may easily slip into the trap of emptying the gospel of its content, accommodating our hearers, and removing the offense inherent in the gospel. To be sure, our own insensitive behavior can add an offense to the gospel that is not properly part of it. We should labor hard to avoid such behavior. But to strip the gospel of those elements that unbelievers find repugnant is not an option.

Martin Luther once remarked that wherever the gospel is preached in its purity, it engenders conflict and controversy. We live in an age that abhors controversy, and we are prone to avoid conflict. How dissimilar this atmosphere is from that which marked the labor of Old Testament prophets and New Testament apostles. The prophets were immersed in conflict and controversy precisely because they would not accommodate the Word of God to the demands of a nation caught up in syncretism. The apostles were engaged in conflict continuously. As much as Paul sought to live peaceably with all men, he found rare moments of peace and little respite from controversy.

That we enjoy relative safety from violent attacks against us may indicate a maturing of modern civilization with respect to religious toleration. Or it may indicate that we have so compromised the gospel that we no longer provoke the conflict that true faith engenders.

Our View of Human Beings

Polls taken by George Barna and George Gallup reveal an alarming intrusion of pagan ideas into the beliefs of modern Christians. A majority of professing evangelicals agree with the statement that human beings are basically good, a clear repudiation of the biblical view of human fallenness. The irony here is that while we decry the baleful influence of secular humanism on the culture, we are busy adopting secular humanism's view of man. It is not so much that the secular culture has negotiated away the doctrine of original sin, as that the evangelical church has done so.

Nowhere do we find more clear evidence of the impact of secularism on Christian thinking than in the sphere of anthropology. Christian anthropology rests not merely on the biblical concept of creation, but on the biblical concept of the fall. Virtually every Christian denomination historically has some doctrine of original sin in its creeds and confessions. These confessional statements do not all agree on the scope or extent of original sin, but they all repudiate everything that would be compatible with humanism. Yet polls show that rank and file evangelicals espouse a view of man more in harmony with humanism than with the Bible and the historic creeds of Christendom.

After the Reformation began in the sixteenth century, one of the earliest books Martin Luther wrote was his highly controversial *The Babylonian Captivity of the Church.* In this volume Luther was sharply critical of the development of sacerdotalism in the Roman Catholic church. He believed that a defective view of the sacraments was leading people away from biblical faith into a foreign gospel.

What would Luther think of the modern heirs of the Reformation? My guess is that he would write on the modern church's captivity to Pelagianism. I think he would see an unholy alliance between Christianity and humanism that reflects more of a Pelagian view of man than the biblical view. This was the germ of his dispute with the Christian humanist Erasmus of Rotterdam.

Though Luther called the doctrine of justification by faith alone *(sola fide)* the "article upon which the church stands or falls," he was convinced that a darker problem was lurking beneath the surface of the debate over justification. He considered his book *The Bondage of the Will (De servo arbitrio)* to be his most important. His debate with Erasmus on the will of fallen people was inseparably related to his understanding of the biblical doctrine of election. Luther called the doctrine of election the *cor ecclesiae,* the "heart of the church."

In Luther's mind the degree of human fallenness is not a trivial matter but strikes at the heart and soul of the Christian life. Luther saw in the work of Erasmus the specter of Pelagius. Despite the historic condemnations of the teaching of Pelagius, it had a strangle hold on the church of Luther's day.

In their "Historical and Theological Introduction" to one edition of Luther's *The Bondage of the Will,* J. I. Packer and O. R. Johnston conclude with a question about the contemporary relevance of the debate:

What is the modern reader to make of *The Bondage of the Will?* That it is a brilliant and exhilarating performance, a masterpiece of the controversialist's difficult art, he will no doubt readily admit; but now comes the question, is Luther's case any part of God's truth? and, if so, has it a message for Christians to-day? No doubt the reader will find the way by which Luther leads him to be a strange new road, an approach which in all probability he has never considered, a line of thought which he would normally label "Calvinistic" and hastily pass by. This is what Lutheran orthodoxy itself has done; and the present-day Evangelical Christian (who has semi-Pelagianism in his blood) will be inclined to do the same. But both history and Scripture, if allowed to speak, counsel otherwise.[1]

Packer and Johnston describe Luther's treatment of the will as a "strange new road" for the modern reader, an approach never considered by present-day evangelicals who have semi-Pelagianism in their blood. This evaluation echoes Roger Nicole's observation that "we are by nature Pelagian in our thinking." Nor does regeneration automatically cure this natural tendency. Even after the Holy Spirit has liberated us from moral bondage, we tend to discount the severity of that bondage.

Packer and Johnston go on to say: "Historically, it is a simple matter of fact that Martin Luther and John Calvin, and, for that matter, Ulrich Zwingli, Martin Bucer, and all the leading Protestant theologians of the first epoch of the Reformation, stood on precisely the same ground here. On other points, they had their differences; but in asserting the helplessness of man in sin, and the sovereignty of God in grace, they were entirely at one. To all of them, these doctrines were the very life-blood of the Christian faith."[2]

The metaphor of "life-blood" is consistent with Luther's metaphor of the "heart" in the *cor ecclesiae*. The Reformers' view of the sinner's moral inability to incline himself toward God's grace was not a secondary or trivial matter to them. In this light they would regard the contemporary evangelical community as suffering from theological hemophilia, in danger of bleeding to death.

We return to Packer and Johnston's introductory essay:

The doctrine of justification by faith was important to them because it safeguarded the principle of sovereign grace; but it actually expressed for them only one aspect of this principle, and that not its deepest aspect. The sovereignty of grace found expression in their thinking at a profounder level still, in the doctrine of monsegistic regeneration—the doctrine, that is, that the faith which receives Christ for justification is itself the free gift of a sovereign God, bestowed by spiritual regeneration in the act of effectual calling. To the Reformers, the crucial question was not simply, whether God justifies believers without works of law. It was the broader question, whether sinners are wholly helpless in their sin, and whether God is to be thought of as saving them by free, unconditional, invincible grace, not only justifying them for Christ's sake when they come to faith, but also raising them from the death of sin by His quickening Spirit in order to bring them to faith. Here was the crucial issue: whether God is the author, not merely of justification, but also of faith; whether, in the last analysis, Christianity is a religion of utter reliance on God for salvation and all things necessary to it, or of self-reliance and self-effort.[3]

Regeneration and Faith

The classic issue between Augustinian theology and all forms of semi-Pelagianism focuses on one aspect of the order of salvation *(ordo salutis):* What is the relationship between regeneration and faith? Is regeneration a monergistic or synergistic work? Must a person first exercise faith in order to be born again? Or must rebirth occur before a person is able to exercise faith? Another way to state the question is this: Is the grace of regeneration operative or cooperative?

Monergistic regeneration means that regeneration is accomplished by a single actor, God. It means literally a "one-working." Synergism, on the other hand, refers to a work that involves the action of two or more parties. It is a co-working. All forms of semi-Pelagianism assert some sort of synergism in the work of regeneration. Usually God's assisting grace is seen as a necessary ingredient, but it is dependent on human cooperation for its efficacy.

The Reformers taught not only that regeneration *does* precede faith but also that it *must* precede faith. Because of the moral bondage of the unregenerate sinner, he cannot have faith until he is changed internally by the operative, monergistic work of the Holy Spirit. Faith is regeneration's fruit, not its cause.

According to semi-Pelagianism regeneration is wrought by God, but only in those who have first responded in faith to him. Faith is seen not as the fruit of regeneration, but as an act of the will cooperating with God's offer of grace.

Evangelicals are so called because of their commitment to the biblical and historical doctrine of justification by faith alone. Because the Reformers saw *sola fide* as central and essential to the biblical gospel, the term *evangelical* was applied to them. Modern evangelicals in great numbers embrace the *sola fide* of the Reformation, but have jettisoned the *sola gratia* that undergirded it. Packer and Johnston assert:

> "Justification by faith only" is a truth that needs interpretation. The principle of *sola fide* is not rightly understood till it is seen as anchored in the broader principle of *sola gratia*. What is the source and status of faith? Is it the God-given means whereby the God-given justification is received, or is it a condition of justification which is left to man to fulfill? Is it a part of God's gift of salvation, or is it man's own contribution to salvation? Is our salvation wholly of God, or does it ultimately depend on something that we do for ourselves? Those who say the latter (as the Arminians later did) thereby deny man's utter helplessness in sin, and affirm that a form of semi-Pelagianism is true after all. It is no wonder, then, that later Reformed theology condemned Arminianism as being in principle a return to Rome (because in effect it turned faith into a meritorious work) and a betrayal of the Reformation (because it denied the sovereignty of God in saving sinners, which was the deepest religious and theological principle of the Reformers' thought). Arminianism was, indeed, in Reformed eyes a renunciation of New Testament Christianity in favour of New Testament Judaism; for to rely on oneself for faith is no different in principle from relying on oneself for works, and the one is as un-Christian and anti-Christian as the other. In the light of what Luther says to Erasmus, there is no doubt that he would have endorsed this judgment.[4]

I must confess that the first time I read this paragraph, I blinked. On the surface it seems to be a severe indictment of Arminianism. Indeed it could hardly be more severe than to speak of it as "un-Christian" or "anti-Christian." Does this mean that

Packer and Johnston believe Arminians are not Christians? Not necessarily. Every Christian has errors of some sort in his thinking. Our theological views are fallible. Any distortion in our thought, any deviation from pure, biblical categories may be loosely deemed "un-Christian" or "anti-Christian." The fact that our thought contains un-Christian elements does not demand the inference that we are therefore not Christians at all.

I agree with Packer and Johnston that Arminianism contains un-Christian elements in it and that their view of the relationship between faith and regeneration is fundamentally un-Christian. Is this error so egregious that it is fatal to salvation? People often ask if I believe Arminians are Christians? I usually answer, "Yes, barely." They are Christians by what we call a felicitous inconsistency.

What is this inconsistency? Arminians affirm the doctrine of justification by faith alone. They agree that we have no meritorious work that counts toward our justification, that our justification rests solely on the righteousness and merit of Christ, that *sola fide* means justification is by Christ alone, and that we must trust not in our own works, but in Christ's work for our salvation. In all this they differ from Rome on crucial points.

Packer and Johnston note that later Reformed theology, however, condemned Arminianism as a betrayal of the Reformation and in principle as a return to Rome. They point out that Arminianism "in effect turned faith into a meritorious work."

We notice that this charge is qualified by the words *in effect.* Usually Arminians deny that their faith is a meritorious work. If they were to insist that faith is a meritorious work, they would be explicitly denying justification by faith alone. The Arminian acknowledges that faith is something a person does. It is a work, though not a meritorious one. Is it a good work? Certainly it is not a bad work. It is good for a person to trust in Christ and in Christ alone for his or her salvation. Since God commands us to trust in Christ, when we do so we are obeying this command. But all Christians agree that faith is something we do. God does not do the believing for us. We also agree that our justification is *by* faith insofar as faith is the instrumental cause of our justification. All the Arminian wants and intends to assert is that man has the ability to exercise the instrumental cause of faith without first being regenerated. This position clearly negates *sola gratia,* but not necessarily *sola fide.*

Then why say that Arminianism "in effect" makes faith a meritorious work? Because the good response people make to the gospel becomes the ultimate determining factor in salvation. I often ask my Arminian friends why they are Christians and other people are not. They say it is because they believe in Christ while others do not. Then I inquire why they believe and others do not? "Is it because you are more righteous than the person who abides in unbelief?" They are quick to say no. "Is it because you are more intelligent?" Again the reply is negative. They say that God is gracious enough to offer salvation to all who believe and that one cannot be saved without that grace. But this grace is cooperative grace. Man in his fallen state must reach out and grasp this grace by an act of the will, which is free to accept or reject this grace. Some exercise the will rightly (or righteously), while others do not. When pressed on this point, the Arminian finds it difficult to escape the conclusion that ultimately his salvation rests on some righteous act of the will he has performed. He has "in effect" merited the merit of Christ, which differs only slightly from the view of Rome.

In concluding their introduction to Luther's *The Bondage of the Will,* Packer and Johnston write:

> These things need to be pondered by Protestants to-day. With what right may we call ourselves children of the Reformation? Much modern Protestantism would be neither owned nor even recognised by the pioneer Reformers. . . . In the light of *[The Bondage of the Will],* we are forced to ask whether Protestant Christendom has not tragically sold its birthright between Luther's day and our own. Has not Protestantism to-day become more Erasmian than Lutheran? Do we not too often try to minimise and gloss over doctrinal differences for the sake of inter-party peace? . . . Have we not grown used to an Erasmian brand of teaching from our pulpits—a message that rests on the same shallow synergistic conceptions which Luther refuted, picturing God and man approaching each other almost on equal terms, each having his own contribution to make to man's salvation and each depending on

the dutiful co-operation of the other for the attainment of that end? . . .[5]

Packer and Johnston call for a modern Copernican revolution in our thinking that would radically change our preaching, our evangelism, and the general life of the church. At issue is the grace and glory of God.

Free Will and Election

When the issue of free will is debated in the modern church, the debate usually focuses on the broader issues of election and predestination. Though these are certainly related matters, they are not exactly the context of the issue between Pelagius and Augustine and later between Erasmus and Luther. The doctrine of election certainly served as the wider issue, but more specifically the issue was the relationship of free will to original sin and to the grace of God.

When free will is debated with reference to predestination, it usually is linked to the sovereignty of God. Can man truly be free if God is sovereign? Some have argued that free will and divine sovereignty are twin truths taught by Scripture that coexist in the tension of an unresolvable dialectic. They are said to transcend all rational attempts to resolve them. They involve a contradiction or at least a severe paradox.

Though the relationship between divine sovereignty and human freedom may be mysterious, they are by no means contradictory. The antithesis to divine sovereignty is not human freedom, but human autonomy. Autonomy represents a degree of freedom that is unlimited by any higher authority or power.

If God is sovereign, then man cannot be autonomous. Conversely if man is autonomous, then God cannot be sovereign. The two are mutually exclusive concepts. Some argue that God's sovereignty is limited by human freedom. If this were the case, then man, not God, would be sovereign. God would always be limited by human decisions and would be lacking in the power or authority to exercise his will over against the creature's. When it is said that God's sovereignty is *limited* by human freedom, however, such a crass view as the one mentioned above is not usually what is intended. Most Christians admit that God has both the power and authority to overrule human decisions. What is intended is that God would never impose his will on the creature by using some sort of coercion. Some speak of a self-limiting of God in such matters. He chooses to limit himself, they say, at the level of human decisions.

Augustinian theology is often charged with reducing man to the level of a puppet whose strings are pulled by the sovereign God. Such a creature can hardly exercise moral responsibility. A puppet is merely a piece of wood whose movements are directed by the strings attached to it. It is not hylozoistic; it has no power or ability to move itself. A puppet cannot think, feel, or respond with affections.

The metaphor of the potter and the clay ceases to be a metaphor and becomes a realistic ontological description. If man is a puppet, he is not substantially different from a piece of clay in a potter's hands. The clay has no will at all. It makes no decisions. It has no conscience. It has no inclinations, morally or otherwise. It is inert and completely passive.

The reality of free will goes to the heart of Christian anthropology. No pun is intended here, but Scripture describes man as having a heart and as being a responsible moral agent. Without a functional will, his moral agency perishes. It is reduced to a sham, a mere chimera with no substantive reality.

On the other side of the equation is the character of God. He is sovereign, but he also has other attributes. His sovereignty does not eclipse his holiness and righteousness. It is a holy sovereignty and a righteous sovereignty. It is this righteousness that concerns those who discuss free will. If man has "no choice" and is merely a passive instrument of divine sovereignty, then it certainly seems that God would be unrighteous to hold creatures responsible for their actions and to punish them for doing what they are powerless not to do.

How we understand the will of man, then, touches heavily on our view of our humanity and God's character. The age-old debate between Pelagianism and Augustinianism is played out in the arena of these issues. Any view of the human will that destroys the biblical view of human responsibility is seriously defective. Any view of the human will that destroys the biblical view of God's character is even worse. The debate will affect our understanding of God's righteousness, sovereignty, and grace. All of these are vital to Christian theology. If we ignore these issues or regard them as trivial, we greatly demean the full character of God as revealed in Scripture. What follows is an historical reconnaissance of the debate over free will as it has played itself out in the history of Christianity.

We, who have been instructed
through the grace of Christ
and born again
to better manhood, . . .
ought to be better than those
who were before the law,
and better also than those
who were under the law.

Pelagius

We Are Capable of Obedience:
Pelagius

elagianism derives its name from a British monk who engaged in a fierce debate with Augustine in the early church. Presumably born in Ireland, Pelagius became a monk and a eunuch. He was stirred in his soul to call the church to a vigorous pursuit of virtue, even of moral perfection. He spent many years in Rome, where he was joined in his struggle with Augustine by Coelestius and by Julian of Eclanum, a bishop who had been widowed as a young man. Of the three, Julian was the more cultured. He was also the most aggressive in the controversy, though he was less an agitator than Coelestius.

Adolph Harnack says Pelagius was "roused to anger by an inert Christendom, that excused itself by pleading the frailty of the flesh and the impossibility of fulfilling the grievous commandments of God." According to Harnack, Pelagius "preached that God commanded nothing impossible, that man possessed the power of doing the good if only he willed, and that the weakness of the flesh was merely a pretext."[1]

The controlling principle of Pelagius's thought was the conviction (noted by Harnack) that God never commands what is impossible for man to perform. This was no abstract theological principle for Pelagius, but a matter that carries urgent practical consequences for the Christian life. He was initially roused against Augustine by a famous prayer Augustine had written: "Grant what thou commandest, and command what thou dost desire."

Pelagius had no quarrel with the latter phrase of this prayer. Indeed it is virtually superfluous. God has a right to command whatever he desires. This is clearly the divine prerogative. The assumption, of course, is that what God desires from his creatures will never be frivolous or evil. This part of Augustine's prayer did not indicate that God needs human permission to legislate his commandments, but reflected instead Augustine's posture of humble submission to the divine right of law.

Pelagius was riled by the first part of Augustine's prayer: "Grant what thou commandest. . . ." What was Augustine asking God to grant? It could not have been his permission, because the creature never needs to ask permission to do what he has been commanded to do. Indeed he would need permission not to do it. Obviously Augustine was asking for something else, some sort of gift to attend the command. Pelagius rightly surmised that Augustine was praying for the gift of divine grace, which would come in the form of some sort of assistance.

Pelagius raised this question: Is the assistance of grace necessary for a human being to obey God's commands? Or can those commands be obeyed without such assistance? For Pelagius the command to obey implies the ability to obey. This would be true, not only of the moral law of God, but also of the commands inherent in the gospel. If God commands people to believe in Christ, then they must have the power to believe in Christ without the aid of grace. If God commands sinners to repent, they must have the ability to incline themselves to obey that command. Obedience does not in any way need to be "granted."

The issue between Pelagius and Augustine was clear. It was not obfuscated by intricate theological arguments, especially in the beginning. "There has never, perhaps, been another crisis of equal importance in Church history in which the opponents have expressed the principles at issue so clearly and abstractly," Harnack says. "The Arian dispute before the Nicene Council can alone be compared with it. . . ."[2]

For Pelagius, nature does not require grace in order to fulfill its obligations. Free will, properly exercised, produces virtue, which is the supreme good and is justly followed by reward. By his own effort man can achieve whatever is required of him in morality and religion.

Events in the Life of Pelagius	
354	Born in Britain
	Became a monk (date, place unknown)
	Resided in Rome (before it fell in 410)
	Converted Coelestius to his views
418	Council at Carthage condemned views of Pelagius and Coelestius
429	Coelestius and possibly Pelagius entered exile in Constantinople
	Death (date, place unknown)

Eighteen Premises

In summarizing the main tenets of Pelagius's thought, I will follow the outline provided by Harnack in his *History of Dogma*. The foundation of Pelagius's thought is the *premise* that God's highest attributes are his goodness and justice. For Pelagius these attributes are the *sine qua non* of the divine character. Without them God would not be God. A God who lacks the perfections of goodness and justice is unthinkable.

The *second premise* on which Pelagius builds is this: If God is altogether good, then everything he has created is likewise good. All of his creation is good, including man. "Adam . . . was created by God sinless, and entirely competent to all good, with an immortal spirit and a mortal body," notes Philip Schaff, summarizing Pelagius's view. "He [Adam] was endowed with reason and free will. With his reason he was to have dominion over irrational creatures; with his free will he was to serve God. Freedom is the supreme good, the honor and glory of man, the *bonum naturae,* that cannot be lost. It is the sole basis of the ethical relation of man to God, who would have no unwilling service. It consists . . .

essentially in the *liberum arbitrium*, or the *possibilitas boni et mali;* the freedom of choice, and the absolutely equal ability at every moment to do good or evil."[3]

Pelagius rooted his view of human nature and free will in his doctrine of creation. Free will consists chiefly in the ability to choose either good or evil. This ability or possibility is the very essence of free will, according to Pelagius. This ability is given to man by God in creation, and it is an essential aspect of man's constituent nature.

Pelagius's *third premise* is that nature was created not only good but inconvertibly good. This is true "because the things of nature persist from the beginning of existence (substance) to its end."[4] Schaff says of Pelagius:

> He views freedom in its *form* alone, and in its *first* stage, and there fixes and leaves it, in perpetual equipoise between good and evil, ready at any moment to turn either way. It is without past or future; absolutely independent of everything without or within; a vacuum, which may make itself a plenum, and then becomes a vacuum again; a perpetual tabula rasa, upon which man can write whatsoever he pleases; a restless choice, which, after every decision, reverts to indecision and oscillation. The human will is, as it were, the eternal Hercules at the cross-road, who takes first a step to the right, then a step to the left, and ever returns to his former position.[5]

If man's will is a perpetual *tabula rasa,* then when a person sins the nature of the will undergoes no change, no deformation. There is no inherent corruption in man. There is no predisposition or inclination to sin that is itself a result of sin. Every act of sin flows from a fresh beginning, a blank tablet that is inscribed with no *a priori* predilection.

The *fourth premise* of Pelagius is that human nature, as such, is indestructibly good. That is, the constituent essence of man remains good. Nature cannot be altered substantively; it can only be modified accidentally. The term *accidentally* here does not mean that something happens unintentionally as a result of misfortune. It refers instead to Aristotle's distinction between an object's substance and its *accidens*. *Accidens* refers to something's external, perceivable qualities, qualities that are on the periphery and are not essential to the thing's being what it is. One's behavior may change when we commit sinful deeds, but these actions do not change one's nature.

Pelagius's *fifth premise,* which follows from the first four, is that evil or sin can never pass into nature. He defines sin as a willingness to do what righteousness forbids, as that from which we are free to abstain and accordingly what we ever and always can avoid by the proper exercise of our will. Sin is always an act and never a nature. Otherwise, Pelagius insisted, God would be the author of evil. Sinful acts can never cause a sinful nature, nor can evil be inherited. If they could, then the goodness and righteousness of God are destroyed.

In his *sixth premise* Pelagius explains that sin exists as the result of Satan's snares and sensuous lust. These enticements to sin can be overcome by the exercise of virtue. Even this lust or concupiscence does not arise from the essence of human nature but is "accidental" to it. This concupiscence is not itself evil, for Christ himself was subject to it. This gives rise to the historic formulation regarding concupiscence: it is of sin and inclines to sin, but itself is not sin.

Pelagius's *seventh premise* concludes that there always remain the possibility and indeed the reality of sinless men. Men can be perfect and some have been. This thesis categorically rejects any doctrine of original sin, that men have a corrupt nature as a result of Adam's fall. This leads to the following theses in which Pelagius describes the status of Adam and his progeny.

The *eighth premise* is that Adam was created with free will and a certain natural holiness. This natural holiness consisted in the freedom of his will and in his reason. Insofar as these faculties were gifts given by God in creation, they can be considered gifts of grace. They were not earned by Adam, but were endowments inherent in his creation.

The *ninth premise* is that Adam sinned by free will. He was not coerced by God or any other creature into committing the first act of sin. This sin did not result in the corruption of his nature. Nor did it result in natural death, because Adam had been created mortal. Adam's sin did result in "spiritual death," which was not a loss of moral ability or an inherent corruption, but the condemnation of the soul on account of sin.

The *tenth premise* is that Adam's progeny inherited from him neither natural death nor spiritual death. His progeny died because they too were mortal. If his progeny suffered spiritual death, it was because they likewise had sinned. They did not suffer spiritual death because of Adam.

Pelagius's *eleventh premise* argued that neither Adam's sin nor his guilt was transmitted to his progeny. Pelagius regarded the doctrine of transmitted sin *(tradux peccati)* and original sin *(peccatum originis)* as a blasphemous theory with roots in Manichaeism. Pelagius insisted it would be unrighteous of God to transmit or impute the sin of one man to others. God would not usher new creatures into a world laden with a burden of sin that was not their own. Original sin would involve changing man's constituent nature from good to bad. Man would become naturally bad. If man were bad by nature either before or after Adam's sin, then God would again be deemed the author of evil. If man's nature became sinful or bad, then it would also be beyond redemption. If original sin is natural, then Christ would have had to possess it and would be unable to redeem himself, let alone anyone else.

Schaff remarks about this dimension of Pelagius's anthropology: "Pelagius, destitute of all idea of the organic wholeness of the race or of human nature, viewed Adam merely as an isolated individual; he gave him no representative place, and therefore his acts no bearing beyond himself. In his view, the sin of the first man consisted in a single, isolated act of disobedience to the divine command. Julian compares it to the insignificant offence of a child, which allows itself to be misled by some sensual bait, but afterwards repents its fault. . . . This single and excusable act of transgression brought no consequences, either to the soul or the body of Adam, still less to his posterity, who all stand or fall for themselves."[6]

For Pelagius there is no connection between Adam's sin and ours. The idea that sin could be propagated via human generation is absurd. "If their own sins do not harm parents after their conversion," Pelagius says, "much more can they not through the parents injure their children."[7]

His *twelfth premise* concluded that all men are created by God in the same position Adam enjoyed before the fall. There are two differences between Adam and his progeny, but these differences are not essential. The first is that Adam was created as an adult; his progeny, as infants. Adam had the full use of reason from the beginning, whereas his progeny had to develop their ability to reason. The second difference is that Adam was set in a garden paradise where there was no prevailing custom of evil; his progeny are born into a society or environment in which the custom of evil prevails. Nonetheless, children are still born sinless.

Why then the virtual universality of sin? Pelagius attributed it to imitation and the long practice of sinning: "For no other cause occasions for us the difficulty of doing good than the long custom of vices, which has infected us from childhood, and gradually, through many years, corrupted us, and thus holds us afterward bound and addicted to itself, so that it seems in some way to have the force of nature."[8]

In this passage Pelagius appears to come close to embracing original sin. The key word, however, is *seems*. Sin does not, in fact, have "the force of nature," despite its widespread presence. In a sense, Pelagius is offering an explanation for why others have been drawn to the idea of original sin.

His *thirteenth premise* is that the habit of sinning weakens the will. This weakening, however, must still be understood in the

Related Works about Pelagius

Harnack, Adolph. *History of Dogma.* Part 2, book 2. Translated by James Millar. 1898. Reprint. New York: Dover, 1961. Pages 168–217.

Pelikan, Jaroslav. *The Christian Tradition: A History of the Development of Doctrine.* Vol. 1, *The Emergence of the Catholic Tradition, 100–600.* Chicago and London: University of Chicago, 1971. Pages 313–18.

Schaff, Philip. *History of the Christian Church.* 8 vols. 1907–10. Reprint. Grand Rapids: Eerdmans, 1952–53. Pages 783–850.

Seeberg, Reinhold. *Text-Book of the History of Doctrines.* Vol. 1, *History of Doctrines in the Ancient Church.* Translated by Charles E. Hay. 1905. Reprint. Grand Rapids: Baker, 1977. Pages 331–57.

accidental sense. The custom of sinning clouds our thinking and leads to bad habits. But these habits describe a practice, not something that actually "inhabits the will." The will is not weakened; it does not undergo a constituent change. It still retains the posture of indifference whenever an ethical or moral decision must be made.

The *fourteenth premise* of Pelagius reveals the beginnings of a concept of grace: Grace *facilitates* goodness. The grace of God makes it easier for us to be righteous. It assists us in our pursuit of perfection. But the crucial point for Pelagius is that, though grace facilitates righteousness, it is by no means essential to attaining righteousness. Man can and should be good without the aid of grace.

"The Pelagian resolution of the paradox of grace was based on a definition of grace fundamentally different from the Augustinian definition, and it was here that the issue was joined," observes Jaroslav Pelikan. "Pelagius was rumored to be 'disputing against the grace of God.' His treatise on grace gave the impression of dwelling 'on scarcely any other topic than the faculty and capacity of nature, while he makes God's grace consist almost entirely in this.' It seemed from this book that 'with every possible argument he defended the nature of man against the grace of God, by which the wicked man is justified and by which we are Christians.'"[9]

Pelagius's *fifteenth premise* declares that the primary grace God gives is that given in creation. This grace is so glorious that some heathens and Jews have achieved perfection.

The *sixteenth premise* denotes the grace given by God in his law, the grace of instruction and illumination. This grace does nothing internally, but yields a clear definition of the nature of goodness. In classic categories of virtue, two distinct things were required: the knowledge of the good and the moral power to do the good. Both are facilitated by the instruction and illumination of the law.

Grace is given, not only by the law, but also, according to the *seventeenth premise*, through Christ. This grace is also defined as *illuminatio et doctrina*. The chief work of Christ is to provide us with an example.

Pelagius writes [in a letter]: "We, who have been instructed through the grace of Christ and born again to better manhood, who have been expiated and purified by his blood, and incited by his example to perfect righteousness, ought to be better than those who were before the law, and better also than those who were under the law"; but the whole argument of this letter, where the topic is simply the knowledge of the law as a means for the promotion of virtue, as well as the declaration, that God opens our eyes and reveals the future "when he illuminates us with the multiform and ineffable gift of celestial grace," proves that for him . . . the "assistance of God" consists, after all, only in instruction.[10]

Pelagius's doctrine of grace is merely the flip-side of his doctrine of sin. Throughout his thought there remains the fundamental assertion of the inconvertibility of human nature. Having been created good, it always and ever remains good.

His final or *eighteenth premise* is that God's grace is compatible with his righteousness. Grace gives no added benefit to the nature of man, but is given by God according to merit. In the final analysis, grace is earned.

We can summarize the eighteen points of Pelagian thought as follows:

1. God's highest attributes are his righteousness and justice.
2. Everything God creates is good.
3. As created, nature cannot be changed essentially.
4. Human nature is indestructibly good.
5. Evil is an act that we can avoid.
6. Sin comes via Satanic snares and sensuous lust.
7. There can be sinless men.
8. Adam was created with free will and natural holiness.
9. Adam sinned through free will.
10. Adam's progeny did not inherit from him natural death.
11. Neither Adam's sin nor his guilt was transmitted.
12. All men are created as Adam was before the fall.
13. The habit of sinning weakens the will.

14. The grace of God facilitates goodness but is not necessary to achieve it.
15. The grace of creation yields perfect men.
16. The grace of God's law illumines and instructs.
17. Christ works chiefly by his example.
18. Grace is given according to justice and merit.

The Course of the Controversy

The Pelagian controversy broke out in either 411 or 412 in Carthage. Pelagius's disciple Coelestius sought to be appointed as presbyter in Carthage. Paulinius brought charges against him, accusing Coelestius of teaching that infant baptism does not aim to cleanse from sin. Harnack lists the points of Paulinius's complaint: Pelagius taught "that Adam was made mortal and would have died whether he had or had not sinned—that Adam's sin injured himself alone, and not the human race—infants at birth are in that state in which Adam was before his falsehood—that the whole human race neither dies on account of Adam's death or falsehood, nor will rise again in virtue of Christ's resurrection—the law admits men to the kingdom of heaven as well as the gospel—even before the advent of our Lord there were impeccable men, *i.e.,* men without sin—that man can be without sin and can keep the divine commands easily if he will."[11]

The Synod of Carthage excommunicated Coelestius. He then retreated to Ephesus, where he succeeded in becoming a presbyter. Meanwhile, Pelagius, desiring to avoid any great controversy, had traveled to Palestine. Pelagius had earlier visited Hippo, but Augustine was away so Pelagius did not meet him. From Jerusalem Pelagius wrote Augustine a flattering letter. Augustine responded with a polite but cautious letter. Augustine was still recovering from the strain of the Donatist controversy, and knew little about the controversy brewing with Coelestius in Carthage. Augustine did receive news from Jerusalem that Pelagius's teachings were causing a stir there.

Orosius, a friend and disciple of Augustine, sought an inquiry against Pelagius in 415, but Pelagius was exonerated. In December of that year a Palestinian synod denounced some of Pelagius's writings. When the synod required him to renounce his teaching that man could be sinless without the aid of grace, Pelagius capitulated. He said, "I anathematize them as foolish, not as heretical, seeing it is no case of dogma." He disclaimed the teaching of Coelestius, saying: "But the things which I have declared to be not mine, I, in accordance with the opinion of the holy church, reprobate, pronouncing an anathema against everyone who opposes."[12]

As a result, Pelagius was pronounced orthodox. Reinhold Seeberg calls Pelagius's answer "a cowardly untruth."[13] This left Pelagius with the difficult task of regaining his credibility with his own supporters. He wrote four books, including *De natura* and *De libero arbitrio,* to elucidate his views.

The North African church was not happy with the results of the synod. Jerome called it a "miserable synod"[14] and Augustine said, "It was not heresy, that was there acquitted, but the man who denied the heresy."[15] Two North African synods were held in 416, and both again condemned Pelagianism. A letter of the proceedings was sent to Pope Innocent, and it was followed by another letter from five North African bishops, including Augustine. Pelagius countered with a letter of his own. Pope Innocent was pleased to be consulted, and he expressed his full agreement with the condemnation of Pelagius and Coelestius: "We declare in virtue of our Apostolic authority that Pelagius and Coelestius are excluded from the communion of the Church until they deliver themselves from the snares of the devil."[16]

In the following year (417) Pope Innocent died and was succeeded by Pope Zosimus. Pelagius sent a well-composed confession of faith to Rome, arguing that he had been falsely accused and misrepresented by his adversaries. In the meantime Coelestius had gone to Rome and submitted to the pope a brief of submission. Augustine's biographer, Peter Brown, writes: "Pelagius hastened to obey the summons of the Roman bishop; he had been preceded by a glowing testimonial from the bishop of Jerusalem. His accusers, the bishops Heros and Lazarus, were personal enemies of Zosimus. . . . In a formal session, Zosimus refused to press Caelestius too far, and so could declare himself satisfied. Pelagius received an even warmer welcome in mid-September. . . . Zosimus told the Africans, '. . . How deeply each one of us was moved! Hardly anyone present could refrain from tears at the thought that persons of such genuine faith could have been slandered.'"[17]

Zosimus's judgment did not conclude the matter. The North African church convened a general council at Carthage in 418 attended by over two hundred bishops. The council issued several canons against Pelagianism, including the following:

> Whosoever says, that Adam was created mortal, and would, even without sin, have died by natural necessity, let him be anathema.
>
> Whoever rejects infant baptism, or denies original sin in children, so that the baptismal formula, "for the remission of sins," would have to be taken not in a strict, but in a loose sense, let him be anathema.
>
> Whoever says, that in the kingdom of heaven, or elsewhere, there is a certain middle place, where children dying without baptism live happy, while yet without baptism they cannot enter into the kingdom of heaven, i.e., into eternal life, let him be anathema.[18]

The canons went on to condemn the following doctrines: "that . . . original sin [is not] inherited from Adam; that grace does not help with reference to future sins; that grace consists only in doctrines and commandments; that grace only makes it easier to do good; [and] that saints utter the fifth petition of the Lord's Prayer not for themselves, or only from humility."[19]

Zosimus then retreated from his earlier position and published an epistle requesting that all bishops subscribe to the canons of this council. Eighteen bishops, including Julian of Eclanum, refused. Historians uniformly regard Julian as the most able and astute defender of Pelagian theology. He pressed his cause with letters to the pope and with a sharp critique of Augustine's views. When Boniface succeeded Zosimus, he urged Augustine to refute

Julian, and this work occupied Augustine until his death. Seventeen of the eighteen bishops who resisted the papal epistle subsequently recanted. Only Julian persisted. After being deposed, he retreated, along with Coelestius, to Constantinople, where in 429 he was welcomed by the patriarch Nestorius. Little is known of the subsequent life of either Pelagius or Coelestius. Julian's alliance with Nestorius did not help him, because Nestorius himself was later condemned for the heresy that bears his name.

The third ecumenical council in Ephesus (A.D. 431), held one year after Augustine's death, condemned Pelagianism. Schaff remarks about the Pelagian system of thought:

> If human nature is uncorrupted, and the natural will competent to all good, we need no Redeemer to create in us a new will and a new life, but merely an improver and ennobler; and salvation is essentially the work of man. The Pelagian system has really no place for the ideas of redemption, atonement, regeneration, and new creation. It substitutes for them our own moral effort to perfect our natural powers, and the mere addition of the grace of God as a valuable aid and support. It was only by a happy inconsistency, that Pelagius and his adherents traditionally held to the church doctrines of the Trinity and the person of Christ. Logically their system led to a rationalistic Christology.[20]

It was by the evil use
of his free-will
that man destroyed
both it and himself.

Augustine

2

We Are Incapable of Obedience:
Augustine

*I*n 1505 Martin Luther entered the monastery in Erfurt. He was ordained in the chapel used by monks of the Augustinian order. When he was ordained neither Luther nor anyone else knew what this event would mean for him, the church, or the world. It was an intersection of time destined to change the course of history forever.

One hundred years earlier the Bohemian reformer Jan Hus had been burned at the stake for heresy. Hus said to the bishop who had ordered his execution, "You may cook this goose, but there will come a swan who will not be silenced." Hus was making a play on words with this prediction. The name *Hus* in the Czech language means "goose."

In the summer of 1996, I led a tour that followed the footsteps of Luther. Celebrations were scheduled all over Germany in commemoration of the 450th anniversary of Luther's death. Posters were widely displayed bearing the likeness of Luther against the backdrop of a swan. The German people saw Luther as the fulfillment of Hus's prophecy, as the incarnate swan who was to come.

The circumstances of Luther's ordination were marked by a double irony. When Luther prostrated himself with arms outstretched in the form of the cross, he was lying at the base of the chapel's altar. The floor was made of stone. The exact spot where Luther lay was marked by an inscription in the stone indicating who was buried directly beneath the spot: the very bishop who had ordered the execution of Jan Hus. It is a great temptation to revise history and ascribe to the bishop an appropriate response to Hus's words that a swan would come. I would like to think the bishop replied, "Over my dead body!" Indeed it was over his dead body that the swan was ordained.

The Augustinian chapel boasted great stained-glass windows featuring great saints of the past. As Luther was prone before the altar, to his left was a large window with a life-sized portrait of Augustine himself. The figure of Augustine is so poised that his eyes are directed downward at the stone floor before the altar. Had Luther lifted his own gaze to the left, he would have looked into the eyes of the patron saint of his order.

The influence of Augustine's thought on Luther is a matter of record. In Luther's account of his famous "tower experience," when he was awakened to the gospel of justification by faith alone, he said this experience was triggered by reading a comment Augustine had written centuries earlier regarding the righteousness of God in Romans 1. The person John Calvin quoted more frequently than any other extra-biblical writer was Augustine. His teaching on grace fueled the Reformation and shaped Protestant theology for centuries. Augustine is generally regarded as the greatest theologian of the first millennium of Christian history, if not of all time.

"The great contribution which Augustine has made to the world's life and thought," says B. B. Warfield, "is embodied in the theology of grace, which he has presented with remarkable clearness and force, vitally in his *Confessions,* and thetically in his anti-Pelagian treatises."[1]

According to Warfield, Augustine established grace as indispensable to the Christian life: "This doctrine of grace came from Augustine's hands in its positive outline completely formulated: sinful man depends, for his recovery to good and to God, entirely on the free grace of God; this grace is therefore indispensable, prevenient, irresistible, indefectible; and, being thus the free grace of God, must have lain, in all the details of its conference and working, in the intention of God from all eternity."[2] Warfield captures the essence of Augustine's central focus on grace.

Events in the Life of Augustine	
354	Born in Tagaste, Numidia, North Africa
371	Began to study rhetoric in Carthage
386	Converted to Christianity
387	Baptized in Milan by Ambrose
391	Ordained a priest in Hippo (North Africa)
396	Became sole Bishop of Hippo
400	Finished writing *Confessions*
412–30	Wrote refutations of Pelagianism
413–26	Wrote *The City of God*
430	Died in Hippo

Augustine seeks to answer the question, What is necessary for fallen man to "recover to good and to God"? How does a creature who is evil recover from this condition and become good? How does a creature who is alienated from God and indisposed toward God find his way back to God? These questions are paramount to an understanding of salvation. For Augustine the answer to them is the grace of God.

This grace is *free* because it is neither merited nor earned. It is *indispensable* because it is the necessary condition for recovery, the *sine qua non* of salvation. It is *prevenient* because it must come *before* the sinner can recover. It is *irresistible* because it is effectual, accomplishing God's purpose in giving it. It is *indefectible* because this liberating grace is perfect, infallible, and unflawed. The gift of grace is linked to God's eternal purpose and is intimately tied to his predestinating purpose.

Augustine's view of grace must be understood against the backdrop of his view of the fall. Immediately we see the sharp contrast between his view of the severity of the fall and that of the Pelagians. He defined mankind as a "mass of sin" *(massa peccati)*.

In *The Enchiridion* Augustine develops his view of the fall:

Through Adam's sin his whole posterity were corrupted, and were born under the penalty of death, which he had incurred.

Thence, after his sin, he was driven into exile, and by his sin the whole race of which he was the root was corrupted in him, and thereby subjected to the penalty of death. And so it happens that all descended from him, and from the woman who had led him into sin, and was condemned at the same time with him—being the offspring of carnal lust on which the same punishment of disobedience was visited—were tainted with the original sin, and were by it drawn through divers errors and sufferings into that last and endless punishment. . . .

Thus, then, matters stood. The whole mass of the human race was under condemnation, was lying steeped and wallowing in misery, and was being tossed from one form of evil to another, and, having joined the faction of the fallen angels, was paying the well-merited penalty of that impious rebellion.[3]

Mankind before the Fall

Augustine affirmed that, as originally created by God, mankind was good and upright. Man's will was both free and good, serving God willingly and with great satisfaction. In *The City of God* Augustine says: "The will, therefore, is then truly free, when it is not the slave of vices and sins. Such was it given us by God; and this being lost by its own fault, can only be restored by Him who was able at first to give it."[4]

In creation, said Augustine, man had the *posse peccare* (the ability to sin), and the *posse non peccare* (the ability not to sin). Even in this state divine assistance was available to him. The "first grace" of which Augustine speaks is that of the so-called *adjutorium*. This gracious assistance enabled Adam to continue in his original state, but did not compel him to persevere in it. Adam had the *posse non peccare* (the ability not to sin), but not the *non posse peccare* (the inability to sin).

These distinctions regarding the creature's moral ability are crucial to understanding Augustine's view of man in creation. God possesses the *non posse peccare*. That is, it is not possible for God to sin. God is not only perfect in his goodness and righteousness, but he is immutably so. The creature is not created immutable. He can and does undergo change. In heaven in our glorified state we will be endowed with the *non posse peccare*. In our glorified state we will be rendered not only sinless but incapable of sinning. But our future incapacity for sin will be not because God will make us divine but because he will preserve us in a state of perfection. In this respect heaven will not be simply a matter of Paradise regained. Heaven will be better than that which Adam enjoyed in Eden prior to the fall.

In creation Adam had the possibility of sinning but not the necessity of sinning. Augustine argues that man not only had the ability not to sin but had the ability to do it easily. Instead he violated the command of God and experienced a horrible fall. Augustine assigns the cause of the fall to pride:

> Our first parents fell into open disobedience because already they were secretly corrupted; for the evil act [would] never [have] been done had not an evil will preceded it. And what is the origin of our evil will but pride? For "pride is the beginning of sin" [Ecclus. 10:13]. And what is pride but the craving for undue exaltation? And this is undue exaltation, when the soul abandons Him to whom it ought to cleave as its end, and becomes a kind of end to itself. This happens when it becomes its own satisfaction. . . . This falling away is spontaneous; for if the will had remained steadfast in the love of that higher and changeless good by which it was illumined to intelligence and kindled into love, it would not have turned away to find satisfaction in itself. . . . The wicked deed, then—that is to say, the transgression of eating the forbidden fruit—was committed by persons who were already wicked.[5]

Augustine does not so much explain the fall as describe it. He identifies the cause of the first transgression as pride. But he recognizes that the presence of pride is already evil. He does not shrink from declaring that the first actual sin was committed by creatures who were already fallen. They fell before they ate the fruit.

When Augustine says the falling away was "spontaneous," he describes the problem but does not explain it. How can a creature with no prior inclination to evil suddenly and spontaneously become so inclined? This is the great poser of the fall, and it remains the most difficult question we continue to face about this event.

Adam's fall affected his moral nature. But not his alone. It also affected that of all his progeny. Here we see the sharp difference between Pelagius and Augustine. Pelagius insisted that Adam's sin affected Adam alone and was not passed on to his descendants except by example. Augustine argued that original sin, as it passes to Adam's progeny, is itself a punishment for sin. All men were seminally in Adam when he was condemned. Those that were "in Adam" were subsequently punished with him.

Augustine, following the Apostle Paul, sees a link between sin and death. All men die because all have sinned. In creation Adam was made with the *posse mori* and the *posse non mori*. This refers to the ability to die and the ability not to die. Adam was not made intrinsically immortal. He would continue to live only as long as he refrained from sin. He could die or not die depending on his response to the command of God. After the fall death entered the world and all of Adam's descendants were placed under its curse. Part of original sin is that fallen man now has the *non posse non mori* (the inability not to die). The special cases of Enoch and Elijah are exceptions made possible only by a special grace given by God.

Augustine had a strong view of the human race's corporate solidarity with Adam. He posited an organic unity of the race, based on Paul's teaching. In *The Enchiridion* Augustine cites Romans 5: "... as by one man sin entered into the world, and death by sin; and so death passed upon all men, for that all have sinned" (Rom. 5:12 KJV). By "the world" Paul here means, of course, the whole human race.

We see then the stark contrast between the thought of Augustine on this point and that of Pelagius and his followers. According to Pelagius, Adam acted as an individual and the consequences of his action were his alone. For Augustine, Adam acted, not as a solitary individual, but as the representative of the human race. He acted vicariously for natural mankind in a way that is analogous to the vicarious work of Christ for redeemed mankind. Augustine writes:

> For we all were in that one man, since we all were that one man, who fell into sin by the woman who was made from him before the sin. For not yet was the particular form created and distributed to us, in which we as individuals were to live, but already the seminal nature was there from which we were to be propagated; and this being vitiated by sin, and bound by the chain of death, and justly condemned, man could not be born of man in any other state. And thus, from the bad use of free will, there originated the whole train of evil, which, with its concatenation of miseries, convoys the human race from its depraved origin, as from a corrupt root, on to the destruction of the second death, which has no end, those only being excepted who are freed by the grace of God.[6]

This concept is fundamental to Augustine's thought, serving as the foundation for the entire doctrine of grace. Since the fall and the subsequent ruination of mankind, only the grace of God can avail for man's redemption.

Related Works by Augustine

The following are found in one or more of the following editions of Augustine's works:

1. *St. Augustin.* 8 vols. In Philip Schaff, ed. *A Select Library of the Nicene and Post-Nicene Fathers of the Christian Church.* First series. Vols. 1–8. 1886–88. Reprint. Grand Rapids: Eerdmans, 1971.
2. *Basic Writings of Saint Augustine.* Edited by Whitney J. Oates. 2 vols. 1948. Reprint. Grand Rapids: Baker, 1980.
3. *Augustine.* 3 vols. Edited by John H. S. Burleigh, Albert C. Outler, and John Burnaby. Library of Christian Classics, edited by John Baillie, John T. McNeill, and Henry P. Van Dusen. Vols. 6–8. London: SCM / Philadelphia: Westminster, 1953–55.

The Enchiridion: On Faith, Hope and Love.
 St. Augustin, 3:237–76.
 Basic Writings, 1:655–730.
 Augustine, 2:335–412.
On Grace and Free Will.
 St. Augustin, 5:435–65.
 Basic Writings, 1:731–74.
On the Grace of Christ and on Original Sin.
 St. Augustin, 5:213–55.
 Basic Writings, 1:581–654.
On the Predestination of the Saints.
 St. Augustin, 5:493–519.
 Basic Writings, 1:775–817.
On the Proceedings of Pelagius.
 St. Augustin, 5:177–212.

Consequences of the Fall

Philip Schaff lists eight distinct consequences of the fall that Augustine developed. We will survey them with comment.

First, *the fall itself.* Since man was created with the *posse peccare,* he had the ability to fall from the beginning. He was created good, but mutably so. This possibility of sinning was later called by Karl Barth an "impossible possibility." This is obviously a nonsense statement, a veritable contradiction of terms. Since Barth was not bothered by contradictions, he found no difficulty in using this phrase. But perhaps Barth deliberately used this jarring contradiction as a literary device to point to the radical incomprehensibility of a good creature falling into sin. The fall is a manifest irrationality.

For Augustine the severity of the fall is seen by its stark contrast to the sublimity of man's original condition. The word *fall* hardly does justice to the idea of a plunge from exalted heights to abysmal depths. Schaff comments: "The fall of Adam appears the greater, and the more worthy of punishment, if we consider, first, the height he occupied, the divine image in which he was created; then, the simplicity of the commandment, and [the] ease of obeying it, in the abundance of all manner of fruits in paradise; and finally, the sanction of the most terrible punishment from his Creator and greatest Benefactor."[7]

The second consequence of sin is *the loss of freedom.* Since this dimension of Augustine's thought is so critical to the entire controversy over free will, we will develop it more fully later. For the moment we note in passing that something disastrous happened to the human will as a result of the fall. In creation man had a positive inclination toward the good and a love for God. Though it was possible for man to sin, there was no moral necessity that he sin. As a result of the fall, man entered into bondage to evil. The fallen will became a source of evil rather than a source for good.

The third consequence of sin is *the obstruction of knowledge.* The intellectual capacity of man was far greater in creation than it was after the fall. The consequences of the fall include what theologians refer to as the "noetic effects of sin." The word *noetic* derives from the Greek word for "mind," which is *nous*. Originally man's mind could absorb and analyze information far better and more accurately than he can now. He could understand truth correctly, without distortion. Man was not, however, endowed by God with the divine attribute of omniscience. This is one of the "incommunicable" attributes that God does not, indeed cannot, "communicate" to a creature. An omniscient being, which has an infinite and eternal grasp of the entire scope of reality, must be eternal and infinite. Therefore Adam had a limit to his endowed knowledge and was on a learning curve from the beginning. His capacity for learning, however, was not obstructed by original sin. In creation the process of learning was facile. Man's mind was not clouded by sin.

After the fall man still possesses a mind. He can still think. He can still reason. He has not lost the faculty of the mind. The faculty remains; the facility is lost. What once was easy is now difficult. Our ability to reason clearly has been affected. We are now prone to muddled thinking and to committing logical errors. We make illegitimate inferences from data and commit logical fallacies. Our arguments are not always sound.

Two major factors are involved here. The first is the weakening of the mind's power and its faculty of thought. The second is the negative influence of sinful bias and prejudice, especially with respect to our understanding of the good and of God. Scripture speaks of our minds being "darkened" and "reprobate." We refuse to have God in our thinking. This is not a mere isolated mental lapse, but a moral lapse in the extreme.

There is an analogy between the function of the mind and the function of the body after the fall. We still have bodies that exhibit physical strength. The body still works. But the work of the body is now attended by sweat and toil. Likewise the mind still works, but correct thinking is laborious for the mind.

The fourth consequence of sin is *the loss of God's grace.* In creation God provided man with an *adjutorium,* a certain gracious assistance for good. After the fall God withdraws this assisting grace from the creature. In a sense man is given over to his sin, to follow the wicked devices of his mind. His heart is now filled with deceit and his desires are only wicked continually. To be sure, there remains a grace by which God, via his law and providence, restrains human evil. He keeps it in check up to a point. But this divine bridle is not the positive assistance of grace to the good but a negative restraint of the evil.

The fifth consequence of sin is *the loss of paradise*. Part of the curse following the fall was banishment from Eden. God expelled Adam and Eve from the garden paradise and posted at the entrance of Eden an angelic sentinel bearing a flaming sword. This sentinel prevented Adam and Eve from reentering the garden. Thus the environment in which they enjoyed God's immediate presence and fellowship was taken away. With exile came also curses on the woman (she would experience pain in childbearing), the serpent (he would crawl on his belly in the dust), and the man (he would, with sweat and toil, work ground that resists his efforts). The new environment is marked by the presence of weeds, thorns, and briars. There were no weeds in the Garden of Eden.

The sixth consequence of sin is *the presence of concupiscence*. The notion of concupiscence, which appears throughout the writings of Augustine, involves a certain predilection for the sensuous. It is not sensuousness itself, but an inclination toward it. It involves a certain "bent" or inclination of the will toward the lusts of the flesh, and this concupiscence wars against the spirit. "Originally the body was as joyfully obedient to the spirit, as man to God," Schaff comments. "There was but one will in exercise. By the fall this beautiful harmony has been broken, and that antagonism has arisen which Paul describes in the seventh chapter of the Epistle to the Romans. . . . *Concupiscentia*, therefore, is substantially the same as what Paul calls in the bad sense 'flesh.' It is not the sensual constitution in itself, but its predominance over the higher, rational nature of man. . . . Concupiscence then is no more a merely corporeal thing than the biblical *sarx*, but has its seat in the soul, without which no lust arises."[8]

The seventh consequence of sin is *physical death*. In creation man had both the *posse mori* and the *posse non mori*, the ability to die or not to die. God warned Adam that if he ate the forbidden fruit, he would die. This warning was denied by the serpent, who claimed that Adam and Eve would not die but become like gods.

We note in passing that God had threatened immediate death: "The day that you eat of it you shall surely die" (Gen. 2:17 NKJV). Yet Adam and Eve did not experience physical death *(thanatos)* on the exact day of their transgression. This has led some to conclude that the "real" penalty for sin was spiritual death, which did ensue immediately. But for the text and for Augustine, the punishment for sin was not limited to spiritual death. It included physical death as well, which Adam and Eve eventually experienced. This was the great enemy that Christ would later conquer for his people. As a result of the fall, physical death is now a necessity, not merely a possibility.

Augustine noted that for Adam and Eve physical death was not totally delayed until they gasped their last breaths. Physical death began the moment they transgressed. From that moment the ravages of death—aging, physical decay, and illness—attended human life. Since the sin of Adam, every baby is born in travail. With the pains of birth and the infant's first cry, the process of death is inaugurated. All of life is part of

Related Works about Augustine

Battenhouse, Roy W. "The Life of St. Augustine." In Roy W. Battenhouse, ed. *A Companion to the Study of St. Augustine.* New York: Oxford University, 1955. Reprint. Grand Rapids: Baker, 1979. Pages 15–56.

Brown, Peter. *Augustine of Hippo: A Biography.* London: Faber and Faber, 1967. Los Angeles: University of California, 1969.

Garcia, Janet, ed. *Christian History* 6, 3 (1987). The entire issue (no. 15) of this popular-level magazine is devoted to Augustine.

Geisler, Norman. *What Augustine Says.* Grand Rapids: Baker, 1982.

Lehman, Paul. "The Anti-Pelagian Writings." In Roy W. Battenhouse, ed. *A Companion to the Study of St. Augustine.* New York: Oxford University, 1955. Reprint. Grand Rapids: Baker, 1979. Pages 203–34.

Sproul, R. C., Jr., ed. *Table Talk* (June 1996). Several articles in this issue of Ligonier Ministries' monthly devotional magazine are devoted to Augustine.

Warfield, Benjamin Breckinridge. "Introduction to Augustine's Anti-Pelagian Writings." In Philip Schaff, ed. *A Select Library of the Nicene and Post-Nicene Fathers of the Christian Church.* First series. Vol. 5, *Saint Augustin: Anti-Pelagian Writings.* 1887. Reprint. Grand Rapids: Eerdmans, 1971. Pages xiii–lxxi. This article was reprinted in Benjamin Breckinridge Warfield, *Studies in Tertullian and Augustine.* New York: Oxford University, 1930. Pages 287–412.

this process. Life marches relentlessly toward the grave. This is the price-tag of sin.

The eighth and final consequence of sin is *hereditary guilt.* *Original sin* means that sin is not merely an action, but also a condition transmitted from our first parents to each of us. Sin is a *habitus,* something that "inhabits" our human nature. This state, condition, or habit of sinfulness continues, through pro-creation, from generation to generation. Is original sin transmit-ted directly through the natural process of human generation? Or does God directly and immediately create each soul afresh? Augustine wavered between these two schools of thought (known as traducianism and creationism) because he thought Scripture does not answer the question definitively.

These consequences of original sin are what Pelagius found so odious. He saw a certain injustice in the progeny of Adam being affected so adversely by Adam's actions. Augustine, on the other hand, regarded original sin as a just punishment for Adam and all whom he represented. He writes in *The City of God:*

> The sin [of our first parents] was a despising of the authority of God. God had created man; had made him in His own image; had set him above the other animals; had placed him in Paradise; had enriched him with abundance of every kind and of safety; had laid upon him neither many, nor great, nor difficult commandments, but, in order to make a wholesome obedience easy to him, had given him a single very brief and very light precept by which He reminded that creature whose service was to be free that He was Lord. Therefore it was just that condemnation followed, and con-demnation such that man, who by keeping the commandments should have been spiritual even in his flesh, became fleshly even in his spirit. And as in his pride he had sought to be his own sat-isfaction, God in His justice abandoned him to himself, not to live in the absolute independence he affected, but instead of the lib-erty he desired, to live dissatisfied with himself in a hard and mis-erable bondage to him to whom by sinning he had yielded him-self. He was doomed in spite of himself to die in body as he had willingly become dead in spirit, condemned even to eternal death (had not the grace of God delivered him) because he had forsaken eternal life. Whoever thinks such punishment either excessive or

unjust shows his inability to measure the great iniquity of sinning where sin might so easily have been avoided.[9]

It is significant that the Pelagian controversy broke out shortly after the Donatist controversy, which involved the issue of baptism. Baptism of infants came to the fore in the Pelagian controversy precisely because the Pelagians insisted that infants are born free of original sin. In the church the baptism for infants was generally considered to involve the remission of sins. Augustine, who supported the notion that baptism related to the forgiveness of original sin and guilt, said of Pelagius: "If you were to ask him what the sin is which he supposes to be remitted to them, he would contend that they had none whatever."

Schaff remarks: "... baptism, according to Augustine, removes only the guilt *(reatus)* of original sin, not the sin itself *(concupiscentia)*. In procreation it is not the regenerate spirit that is the agent, but the nature which is still under the dominion of the *concupiscentia.* 'Regenerate parents produce not as sons of God, but as children of the world.'"[10]

The doctrine of original sin is central to Augustine's understanding of both grace and free will. Original sin makes grace necessary. Original sin defines the bondage of the will. One's view of grace and free will is inseparably related to one's understanding of original sin. He who embraces Augustine's view of original sin is compelled to probe his understanding of grace and the fallen will.

The Nature of Free Will

Augustine understood the will to be a faculty that is part of the constituent nature given to man in creation. It makes man a volitional creature and makes it possible for him to be a moral creature. Creatures who lack minds or wills cannot be moral beings. To be capable of moral action, either virtue or vice, a being must be able to make moral choices. For example, when a drop of rain falls to the ground, we do not regard this as a moral falling. A fall from the sky is not a fall from righteousness.

Later philosophers such as Gottfried Leibniz distinguished between several types of evil, such as metaphysical evil, physical evil, and moral evil. Metaphysical "evil" refers to finitude or the lack of pure being (like that found in God).

Physical "evil" refers to natural disasters like floods or earthquakes. We think of such events as bad, but we do not attribute moral culpability to the water that floods or the earth that shakes.

Moral evil refers to the actions of volitional creatures. Augustine regarded man as fallen and as a sinner, but he did not mean that in the fall man had lost his moral agency. Indeed, it is precisely because man remains a volitional being that he is culpable for sin. "There is . . . always within us a free will—but it is not always good," Augustine says. "For it is either free from righteousness when it serves sin—and then it is evil—or else it is free from sin when it serves righteousness—and then it is good."[11]

Augustine clearly affirms that man before and after the fall possesses free will. The ability to choose, or the faculty of the will, remains in man even after the fall. Augustine insists we "always" have a free will. The direction of the will, however, may be to either good or evil. We can have a good free will or an evil free will. This distinction goes to the core of Augustine's thought. Schaff notes:

> By freedom Augustine understands, in the first place, simply *spontaneity* or *self-activity*, as opposed to action under external constraint or from animal instinct. Both sin and holiness are *voluntary*, that is, acts of the will, not motions of natural necessity. This freedom belongs at all times and essentially to the human will, even in the sinful state (in which the will is, strictly speaking, *self-*willed); it is the necessary condition of guilt and punishment, of merit and reward. In this view no thinking man can deny freedom, without destroying the responsibility and the moral nature of man. An involuntary will is as bald a self-contradiction as an unintelligent intelligence.[12]

Augustine defined *free will* as the ability to make voluntary decisions free from external constraint or coercion. It is self-activity. *Self-activity* refers to actions caused by the self, not to actions caused by external force. It is active, not passive. The person is not an inert object or a passive puppet. This freedom is a necessary condition or prerequisite for moral behavior of any kind.

At times Augustine seems to deny all freedom to the will of fallen man. In *The Enchiridion,* for example, he writes: ". . . when man by his own free-will sinned, then sin being victorious over him, the freedom of his will was lost."[13]

How can we square this statement with Augustine's insistence elsewhere that man always has freedom of the will? Some critics of Augustine think that anyone who attempts to resolve this difficulty is on a fool's errand. They assert that Augustine simply hardened his position in his later years in light of the Pelagian crisis and contradicted his earlier teaching.[14]

To square the problem let us look at two matters. The first is Augustine's crucial distinction between *free will (liberum arbitrium)* and *liberty (libertas).* In our use of language we normally consider the terms *liberty* and *freedom* to be virtually synonymous. For Augustine that was not the case. When he speaks of free will, he means the ability to choose without external constraint.

The sinner sins because he chooses to sin, not because he is forced to sin. Without grace the fallen creature lacks the ability to choose righteousness. He is in bondage to his own sinful impulses. To escape this bondage the sinner must be liberated by the grace of God. For Augustine the sinner is both free and in bondage at the same time, but not in the same sense. He is free to act according to his own desires, but his desires are only evil. In an ironic sense he is a slave to his own evil passions, a slave to his own corrupted will. This corruption greatly affects the will, but it does not destroy it as a faculty of choosing.

We must also examine the broader context in which Augustine said that the freedom of the will is lost in the fall. The larger text in *The Enchiridion* reads:

> . . . it was by the evil use of his free-will that man destroyed both it and himself. For, as a man who kills himself must, of course, be alive when he kills himself, but after he has killed himself ceases to live, and cannot restore himself to life; so, when man by his own free-will sinned, then sin being victorious over him, the freedom

of his will was lost. "For of whom a man is overcome, of the same is he brought in bondage" [2 Peter 2:19 KJV]. This is the judgment of the Apostle Peter. And as it is certainly true, what kind of liberty, I ask, can the bond-slave possess, except when it pleases him to sin? For he is freely in bondage who does with pleasure the will of his master. Accordingly, he who is the servant of sin is free to sin. And hence he will not be free to do right, until, being freed from sin, he shall begin to be the servant of righteousness. And this is true liberty, for he has pleasure in the righteous deed; and it is at the same time a holy bondage, for he is obedient to the will of God. But whence comes this liberty to do right to the man who is in bondage and sold under sin, except he be redeemed by Him who has said, "If the Son shall make you free, ye shall be free indeed" [John 8:36 KJV]? And before this redemption is wrought in a man, when he is not yet free to do what is right, how can he talk of the freedom of his will and his good works, except he be inflated by that foolish pride of boasting which the apostle restrains when he says, "By grace are ye saved, through faith" [Eph. 2:8 KJV].[15]

Augustine is answering his own question, Can a man be restored from his fallen condition by the free determination of his own will? He answers, "God forbid." Once a man commits suicide, he is powerless to restore himself to life. Augustine makes an analogy between physical (biological) death and spiritual death. The man who is spiritually dead is still biologically alive. He remains human. He still makes choices. But he is spiritually dead, and his choices are spiritually bankrupt. The fallen sinner is "freely in bondage." The point is simple. The servant of sin serves his master willingly. He "does with pleasure the will of his master." The sinner still has a "kind of liberty": the ability to choose the sin he takes pleasure in doing.

Augustine contrasts the "freedom" of the bond-servant with "true liberty," which consists in having pleasure in the righteous deed. Again he uses paradox by calling true liberty a "holy bondage." This is not unlike the teaching of Christ, who declared that we must become servants in order to be free, or the teaching of Paul, who declared his liberty as a bond-servant of Christ.

In his essay on free will, Augustine identified pleasure or desire *(libido)* as the crucial element in the will's bondage to sin. The sinner chooses what he desires or what is pleasing to him. In this sense the sinner is still free to do what he wants to do. But because he has no desire for righteousness, he is in spiritual bondage. He is in bondage to himself, to his own sinful desires.

Reinhold Seeberg summarizes Augustine at this point: "Yet, despite all this, we may speak of a free will *(liberum arbitrium)* even in the case of the sinner, though not in the sense of the Pelagian *possibilitas utriusque partis,* for a man cannot be at the same time both a good and an evil tree. The *libertas* of paradise has been lost, *i.e.* 'to have with righteousness full immortality'; for this freedom ('free to live well and uprightly') now exists only by virtue of the influence of 'grace,' which is precisely what is lacking in the sinner's case."[16]

Grace and Liberty

For the sinner to move from bondage to liberty, God must exercise his grace. In *The Enchiridion* Augustine said that before man is redeemed, he is not yet free to do what is right. That ability comes by grace through faith. Augustine then labors the point that liberty does not come from the action of one who is in bondage to sin. The sinner does not first choose to believe, then experience liberation. The faith that liberates is itself a gift. Augustine declares not only that faith is a gift (citing Eph. 2:8), but also that true liberty is likewise a gift of divine grace. It is God who prepares the heart to believe. Augustine writes: ". . . the true interpretation of the saying, 'It is not of him that willeth, nor of him that runneth, but of God that showeth mercy' [Rom. 9:16], is that the whole works belongs to God, who both makes the will of man righteous, and thus prepares it for assistance, and assists it when it is prepared."[17]

Augustine's view is frequently said to be that God saves people who are unwilling to be saved, or that his grace operates against their wills, forcing them to choose and bringing them into the kingdom "kicking and screaming against their will." This is a gross distortion of Augustine's view. The grace of God operates on the heart in such a way as to make the formerly unwilling sinner willing. The redeemed person chooses Christ because he wants to choose Christ. The person now wills Christ because God has created a new spirit within the person. God makes the will righteous by removing the hardness of the heart and converting an opposing will. "...if God were not able to remove from the human heart even its obstinacy and hardness," Augustine says, "He would not say, through the prophet, 'I will take from them their heart of stone, and will give them a heart of flesh'" [Ezek. 11:19].[18]

Augustine's view of the grace that liberates is linked to his view of predestination. He argues that God converts bad wills to good wills.[19] He does this for the elect. Eschewing any view of election based on God's foreknowledge of who will believe, Augustine writes: "Let us, then, understand the calling whereby they become elected—not those who are elected because they have believed, but who are elected that they may believe."[20]

Pelagius understood election to mean that God "foreknew who would be holy and immaculate by the choice of free will, and on that account elected them before the foundation of the world in that same foreknowledge of His in which He foreknew that they would be such. Therefore He elected them...."[21] Over against this, Augustine insisted that election and predestination are unto holiness. "When, therefore, He predestinated us, He foreknew His own work by which He makes us holy and immaculate," Augustine says. "He, therefore, worketh the beginning of our belief who worketh all things; because faith itself does not precede that calling.... For He chose us, not because we believed, but that we might believe.... Neither are we called because we believed, but that we may believe; and by that calling which is without repentance it is effected and carried through that we should believe."[22]

*If anyone says
that man's free will
  [when] moved and aroused by God,
by assenting to God . . .
in no way cooperates . . .
  [and] that it cannot refuse its assent
if it wishes, . . .
let him be anathema!*

Council of Trent

3

We Are Capable of Cooperating:
Semi-Pelagians

hough the Pelagian controversy ended with the condemnation of Pelagius and his followers, the views of Augustine were
not universally accepted in all their details. At first, opposition
arose to some elements of Augustine's thought in North Africa.
Some monks from the monastery of Adrumetum in North Africa
objected to Augustine's view of predestination and to his view
that fallen man is morally unable to incline himself to the grace
of God. Questions arising from this debate prompted Augustine
to write *On Grace and Free Will* and *On Rebuke and Grace.* These
works were answered by the abbot of the monastery, Valentinus,
in a cordial and respectful manner.

As discussion continued in North Africa, a more violent opposition to Augustine's views erupted in France, particularly in the
south at Massilia. Friends of Augustine, Hilary and Prosper,

reported to him this opposition and urged him to write a response. Augustine did so in his final two works, *On the Predestination of the Saints* and *On the Gift of Perseverance.* In these works Augustine dealt more gently with his critics than he did with Pelagius, regarding them as brothers in the faith. This attitude anticipates the aura of future controversies. In the main, both Augustinians and semi-Pelagians tend to regard Pelagianism as a heresy so serious that it is non-Christian, while the on-going controversy between Augustinianism and semi-Pelagianism is an intramural debate among believers. Though the issues involved are deemed to be quite serious by both sides, they are not regarded to be so serious as to be essential to Christian faith.

The leading spokesman of the semi-Pelagian party was John Cassian, abbot of the monastery of Massilia. He is so identified with semi-Pelagianism that it is sometimes called Cassianism. Cassian bowed before the inscrutable mystery of God's decrees and was reluctant to probe deeply into the question of predestination. His chief concern was to safeguard the universality of God's grace and the real moral accountability of fallen man.

When a theological controversy arises, it is wise to back off for a moment and ask, "What are the concerns?" By focusing on the concerns of both parties in a dispute, we create an atmosphere in which both sides can be fairly heard. Both sides often discover that they share common concerns but have different ways of dealing with them or stress different areas of importance. For example, Augustine clearly had a strong desire to maintain the primacy of divine grace and sovereignty. The semi-Pelagians wanted to preserve the same truths, but they were also deeply concerned about human freedom and responsibility, as well as the universal availability of saving grace.

When mutual concerns are stated and even when both sides share certain concerns, this does not automatically resolve the issues. Finding points of agreement can improve the atmosphere of the discussion and provide a basis for mutual trust between the disputants. But then the discussion must proceed finally to the issues on which the parties differ.

The Semi-Pelagianism of Cassian

The concerns of Cassian and his supporters include the following:

1. Augustine's views are new and represent a departure from the teachings of the church fathers, especially Tertullian, Ambrose, and Jerome. Cassian himself was a student of Chrysostom.
2. Augustine's teaching on predestination "cripples the force of preaching, reproof, and moral energy, . . . plunges men into despair," and introduces "a certain fatal necessity."[1]
3. Augustine's strong views are unnecessary to refute and escape the heresies of Pelagius.
4. Though God's grace is necessary for salvation and assists the human will in doing good, it is man, not God, who must will that which is good. Grace is given "in order that he who has begun to will may be assisted," not to give "the power to will."[2]
5. God desires to save all people, and the propitiation of Christ's atonement is available to all.
6. Predestination is based on divine foreknowledge.
7. There is not "a definite number of persons to be elected or rejected," since God "wishes all men to be saved, and yet not all men are saved."[3]

Cassian wrote twelve books probing the struggles and virtues of monastic life. In *Collationes patrum* he details his differences with both Pelagius and Augustine. "In this work, especially in the thirteenth Colloquy, he rejects decidedly the errors of Pelagius, and affirms the universal sinfulness of men, the introduction of it by the fall of Adam, and the necessity of divine grace to every individual act," Philip Schaff writes. "But, with evident reference to Augustine, though without naming him, he combats the doctrines of election and of the irresistible and particular operation of grace, which were in conflict with the church tradition, especially with the Oriental theology, and with his own earnest ascetic legalism."[4]

Cassian emphasized the reality of both human sinfulness and man's moral responsibility. He maintained that Adam's sin is a hereditary disease. Since the fall of Adam there has been an *infirmitas liberi arbitrii*.[5] Cassian affirms a doctrine of original sin in which man is fallen in Adam. Even Adam's free will was infected by the fall, at least to the degree that it is now "infirm." The will is not destroyed, nor is it completely impotent morally. Here Cassian rejects Augustine's view of the will's moral inability to incline itself to good or to God.

Over against Pelagius, Cassian insisted that grace is necessary for righteousness. This grace, however, is resistible. For it to be effective the human will must cooperate with it. Cassian is primarily concerned here to maintain that we are unable to do any good without God's help and that our free will must be active.

Adolph Harnack summarizes Cassian's view:

> God's grace is the foundation of our salvation; every beginning is to be traced to it, in so far as it brings the chance of salvation and the possibility of being saved. But that is external grace; inner grace is that which lays hold of a man, enlightens, chastens, and sanctifies him, and penetrates his will as well as his intelligence. Human virtue can neither grow nor be perfected without this grace—therefore the virtues of the heathens are very small. But the *beginnings* of the good resolve, good thoughts, and faith—understood as the preparation for grace—can be due to ourselves. Hence grace is absolutely necessary in order to reach final salvation (perfection), but not so much so in order to make a start. It accompanies us at all stages of our inner growth, and our exertions are of no avail without it *(libero arbitrio semper co-operatur);* but it only supports and accompanies him who really strives. . . . even this . . . action of grace is not irresistible.[6]

In Cassian's view his key difference with Augustine was over irresistible grace. For Augustine, man's will, though still capable of making choices, is morally unable to incline itself toward good. The will is not spiritually infirm, but spiritually dead. Only the effectual grace of God can liberate the sinner to believe. The difference between Augustine and Cassian is the difference between monergism and synergism at the beginning of salvation. Cassian and semi-Pelagianism is, with respect to the sinner's initial step toward salvation, decidedly synergistic. God makes his grace available to the sinner, but the sinner must, with his infirm will, cooperate with this grace in order to have faith or to be regenerated. Faith precedes regeneration. For Augustine the grace of regeneration is monergistic. That is, the divine initiative is a necessary precondition for faith.

When Augustine says grace is irresistible, he means it is effectual. It is a monergistic work of God that accomplishes what he intends it to accomplish. Divine grace changes the human heart, resurrecting the sinner from spiritual death to spiritual life. Regenerating grace makes the sinner willing to believe and come to Christ. Formerly the sinner was unwilling and not inclined to choose Christ, but now he is not only willing but eager to choose Christ. The sinner is not dragged to Christ against his will or forced to choose something he does not want to choose. The grace of divine regeneration changes the heart's disposition in such a way as to raise the sinner from death to life, from unbelief to faith.

This view is clearly monergistic *at* the initial point of the sinner's movement from unbelief to faith. The whole process, however, is not monergistic. Once the operative grace of regeneration is given, the rest of the process is synergistic. That is, after the soul has been changed by effectual or irresistible grace, the person himself chooses Christ. God does not make the choice for him. It is the person who believes, not God who believes for him. Indeed the rest of the Christian life of sanctification unfolds in a synergistic pattern.

There is much confusion about the debate between monergism and synergism. When Augustinianism is defined as monergistic, one must remember that it is monergistic with respect to the beginning of salvation, not to the whole process. Augustinianism does not reject *all* synergism, but does reject a synergism that is *all synergism.*

On the other hand, semi-Pelagianism is *all synergism.* That is, it is synergistic *from the beginning.* Reinhold Seeberg comments:

The idea of Cassian is, that the human will has indeed been crippled by sin, but that a certain freedom has yet remained to it. By virtue of this, it is able to turn to God, and, just as though God had first turned to it, it is able, with the assistance of divine grace, setting before it the law and infusing the needed power, to will and to do that which is good. Hence the sinner is not dead, but wounded. Grace comes to view, not as *operans,* but as *cooperans;* to it is to be attributed not alone-activity, but synergy. . . . It was an instructive attempt to preserve the personal and spiritual relationship of man to God. But the attempt of necessity surrendered that which was the best in Augustine—the *sola gratia.*[7]

A similar summary is offered by Schaff:

In opposition to both systems [Pelagianism and Augustinianism] he [Cassian] taught that the divine image and human freedom were not annihilated, but only weakened, by the fall; in other words, that man is sick, but not dead, that he cannot indeed help himself, but that he can desire the help of a physician, and either accept or refuse it when offered, and that he must co-operate with the grace of God in his salvation. The question, which of the two factors has the initiative, he answers, altogether empirically, to this effect: that sometimes, and indeed usually, the human will, as in the cases of the Prodigal Son, Zaccheus, the Penitent Thief, and Cornelius, determines itself to conversion; sometimes grace anticipates it, and, as with Matthew and Paul, draws the resisting will—yet, even in this case, without constraint—to God. Here, therefore, the *gratia praeveniens* is manifestly overlooked.[8]

Schaff is a bit imprecise when implying that Augustine teaches that the fall "annihilated" human freedom. We remember Augustine's distinction between freedom (free will) and liberty. Free will was not annihilated in the sense that the will was obliterated or destroyed. What was annihilated is the moral power to incline to the good. Liberty was annihilated, according to Augustine, not free will.

For Cassian, the grace God provides the sinner, with which the sinner must cooperate to be saved, is chiefly the grace of

Fig. 3.1
Controversy in the Fifth Century

Augustinians			Semi-Pelagians		
Augustine	354–	430	John Cassian	360–	435
Prosper of Aquitane	c. 390–c. 463		Faustus of Riez	c.400–c. 490	

illumination or instruction. Conversion is effected in this way: ". . . when he has observed in us a certain beginning of a good will, [God] immediately illuminates this and comforts and incites it toward salvation, bestowing an increase upon that which either he himself has implanted or which he has seen to arise from our own effort."[9] The crucial point is that the beginning of salvation depends on the initial stirring of a good will within the fallen sinner. God gives the assistance of grace to those who make such a good beginning. For Augustine, no sinner can make such a good beginning unless God first liberates him.

Resistance to Semi-Pelagianism

Against the work of Cassian, Augustine's friend Prosper of Aquitaine wrote a book on grace and freedom in 432. Cassian gained allies in the monk Vincent of Lerins, Faustus of Riez, Gennadius of Massilia, and Arnobius. The debate continued to rage for decades. Semi-Pelagianism gained victory in Gaul in the Synods of Arles (472) and Lyons (475). In the meantime, Augustinianism was being somewhat softened by Augustine's successors. In 496 Pope Gelasius I sanctioned the writings of Augustine and Prosper and condemned those of Cassian and Faustus. The debate reached its climax in 529 at the Synod of Orange, which condemned the system of semi-Pelagianism.

Schaff provides a list of the crucial propositions set forth by the church at the Synod of Orange:

- The sin of Adam has not injured the body only, but also the soul of man.
- The sin of Adam has brought sin and death upon all mankind.
- Grace is not merely bestowed when we pray for it, but grace itself causes us to pray for it.
- Even the beginning of faith, the disposition to believe, is effected by grace.
- All good thoughts and works are God's gift.
- Even the regenerate and the saints need continually the divine help.
- What God loves in us, is not our merit, but his own gift.
- The free will weakened in Adam, can only be restored through the grace of baptism.
- All good that we possess is God's gift, and therefore no one should boast.
- When man sins, he does his own will; when he does good, he executes the will of God, yet voluntarily.
- Through the fall free will has been so weakened, that without prevenient grace no one can love God, believe on Him, or do good for God's sake. . . .
- In every good work the beginning proceeds not from us, but God inspires in us faith and love to Him without merit precedent on our part, so that we desire baptism, and after baptism can, with His help, fulfil His will.[10]

Clearly the Roman Catholic church was rejecting the view that the beginning point of faith is the fallen will. The ability to do good proceeds from grace, the grace imparted by regeneration. It must be noted that here, as well as in Augustine, the grace of regeneration is effected by the sacrament of baptism. Baptismal regeneration was later rejected categorically by Calvinists as well as most other Protestants.

Predestination and irresistible grace were more or less passed over in the synod's pronouncements. The church embraced a way that was more Augustinian than Pelagian. Some have referred to it as semi-Augustinianism rather than semi-Pelagianism, finding it closer to Augustine than to Cassian.

Ambiguity at the Council of Trent

In the sixteenth century the Protestant Reformation raised the issues of Pelagianism and semi-Pelagianism afresh. The response of the Roman Catholic church at the Council of Trent sheds light on how these issues had developed. In the council's sixth session the church defined its doctrine of justification and listed canons against various views the church deemed to be heretical. The first three canons clearly reiterate the church's historic repudiation of pure Pelagianism. Canons 4 and 5 leave some ambiguity with respect to semi-Pelagianism.

Canon 4 of the sixth session reads: "If anyone says that man's free will [when] moved and aroused by God, by assenting to God's call and action, in no way cooperates toward disposing and preparing itself to obtain the grace of justification, [and] that it cannot refuse its assent if it wishes, but that, as something inanimate, it does nothing whatever and is merely passive, let him be anathema."[11]

The ambiguity here is complex. The first assertion is that man cooperates by assenting to God when God moves and excites the will. But what does it mean that the will is "moved and aroused by God"? Augustinian theology affirms that after God changes the disposition of the will by his grace, the sinner cooperates and assents to God's will. This assent, however, is a result of God's monergistic operation on the sinner's enslaved will. The Reformers might even agree that the will disposes and prepares itself for the grace of *justification* (not regeneration), but it is unlikely they would have used this language. Such terminology leaves open the critical question vis-à-vis semi-Pelagianism: Does the will, prior to regeneration, ever dispose or prepare itself for grace?

The council added confusion when it denied that the will cannot dissent even if it should want to. This statement is strange because it clearly misses the mark. As we will see later, the Reformers did not teach that God's irresistible grace makes people unable to dissent even if they should want to. The effectual work of God is such that the sinner cannot dissent precisely because he does not want to dissent. He cannot choose to do what he does not choose to do. Nor does the Augustinian view regard the fallen will as an inanimate thing, though it is passive at the moment it receives the grace of regeneration.

Lutheran theologian Martin Chemnitz looks to Jacob Payva Andrada for the definitive interpretation of this canon: "He explains the opinion, both the synod's [or council's] and his own, thus: That free will, without the inspiration and assistance of the Spirit cannot indeed bring about spiritual actions but that this does not happen for this reason, that the mind and will, such as it is in man from the very moment of birth, does not before his conversion have any strength, any powers or faculties whatever which are necessary for beginning and effecting spiritual actions, but because these natural powers and faculties, although they have neither been destroyed nor extinguished, have been so entangled in the snares of sins that man cannot extricate himself from them by his own strength."[12]

Here we see that the council clearly denied Pelagianism by affirming that the fallen person can do no spiritual good without the assistance of grace. But the question remains, what moral ability does the unregenerate person have to respond to the assistance of grace? Chemnitz continues:

> . . . the Tridentine Council . . . says that free will freely assents and cooperates with the inciting and assisting grace of God. For they are of the opinion that in the mind and will of the unregenerate man there are still from the moment of his birth in this corruption some naturally implanted powers, or some kind of faculties, for divine things or spiritual actions, but that the movement and use of those faculties and powers is repressed and retarded through sin in the unregenerate. So they are of the opinion that the grace of God and the working of the Spirit do not simply effect and work in those who are born again some new power, strength, faculty, or ability of beginning and performing spiritual impulses and action which before conversion and renewal they did not have from the powers of nature, but that they only break the fetters and are set free from the snares so that the natural faculty, previously bound, restrained, and hindered, can now, incited through grace, exercise its powers in spiritual matters.[13]

If Chemnitz is correct, then Trent both reaffirmed the church's condemnation of Pelagianism and retreated from a clear condemnation of semi-Pelagianism. The council essentially adopted the semi-Pelagian view of the will and original sin.

Canon 5 of the sixth session declares: "If anyone says that after the sin of Adam man's free will was lost and destroyed, or that it is a thing only in name, indeed a name without a reality, a fiction introduced into the Church by Satan, let him be anathema."[14]

Again, it is difficult to discern the target of this canon. Augustine and the Reformers taught that man's free will was not extinguished by the fall. What was extinguished, according to Augustine, was liberty, the moral ability to do good.

John Calvin's response to Trent's teaching is similar to that of Chemnitz. To the first three canons' anti-Pelagianism, Calvin simply says, "Amen." With respect to Canon 4 he writes: "We certainly obey God with our will, but it is with a will which he has formed in us. Those, therefore, who ascribe any proper movement to free-will, apart from the grace of God, do nothing else than rend the Holy Spirit. Paul declares, not that a faculty of willing is given to us, but that the will itself is formed in us (Phil. 2:13), so that from none else but God is the assent or obedience of a right will. He acts within, holds our hearts, moves our hearts, and draws us by the inclinations which he has produced in us. So says Augustine. What preparation can there be in a heart of iron, until by a wondrous change it begins to be a heart of flesh?"[15]

Calvin's remarks take on an even sharper tone when he responds to Canon 5:

Let us not raise a quarrel about a word. But as by Free-will they understand a faculty of choice perfectly free and unbiassed to either side, those who affirm that this is merely to use a name without a substance, have the authority of Christ when he says, that they are free whom the Son makes free, and that all others are the slaves of sin. Freedom and slavery are certainly contrary to each other. As to the term itself, let them hear Augustine, who maintains that the human will is not free so long as it is subject to passions which vanquish and enthral it. Elsewhere he says, "The will being vanquished by the depravity into which it has fallen, nature is without freedom." Again, "Man, making a bad use of free-will, lost both himself and it."[16]

Again we see the play on the words *freedom, free,* and *free will.* Elsewhere Calvin, like Augustine, allowed for free will in the sense that the sinner does not act by external compulsion. The will is not free inwardly in the moral sense, however, because it is in bondage to evil inclinations.

Both Chemnitz (a Lutheran) and Calvin saw in Trent a departure from the Augustinian view of the will. Later events in the church tend to confirm their judgment.

The Augustinianism of Jansen

Further developments within the Roman Catholic church toward the end of the sixteenth century prepared the way for the Jansenist controversy of the seventeenth. Michael Baius, a professor in Louvain, strongly asserted the Augustinian doctrines of grace. He argued that man is utterly depraved by sin: "Free-will without the assistance of God avails for nothing except for sin."[17] Justification is gained only after the sinner's will has been transformed by God. Seventy-nine theses of Baius were condemned in a bull issued by Pope Pius V. Among the theses condemned were such Augustinian ideas as: (1) the will without grace can only sin; (2) even the concupiscence that is contrary to the will is sin; and (3) the sinner is moved and animated by God alone.

Jesuit theologian Luis de Molina sought to achieve a synthesis by which Pelagianism, semi-Pelagianism, and Augustinianism could be reconciled. Seeberg summarizes his views: "Man is, even in his sinful state, free to perform, not only natural, but also supernatural works, the cooperation of grace being presupposed. Grace elevates and stimulates the soul . . . but the real act of decision is not wrought in the will by grace, but is made by the will itself, the will being, however, in union with grace. . . . Now the thorough-

Fig. 3.2

Controversy in the Sixteenth and Seventeenth Centuries

Augustinians		Semi-Pelagians	
John Calvin	1509–1564	Council of Trent	1545–1563
Martin Chemnitz	1522–1586		
		Luis de Molina	1535–1600
Cornelis Jansen	1585–1640		
Pasquier Quesnel	1634–1719		
Blaise Pascal	1623–1662		

going cooperation thus attained becomes a mere illusion if all the free acts of created beings are really recognized, as among the Thomists, as willed by God himself of his own original motion."[18]

With respect to predestination and election, Luis adopted a prescient view (based on his theory of "median knowledge") according to which God's election rests on his foreknowledge of free human choices. "It is true, a critical eye will readily discover that the combination thus assumed is only apparent, and that the Augustinian-Thomistic conception of grace is here torn out by its roots," Seeberg writes. "Synergism in its boldest form is the confessed first principle of this theology. But the opposition to it inaugurated by the Dominicans was crippled by the championship of the Jesuits, who adopted this theory of grace as the official doctrine of their order."[19]

The dispute between the Dominicans and Jesuits resulted in an appeal to the pope. But no papal declaration was forthcoming, leaving the Jesuits to continue teaching the Molinist position without ecclesiastical opposition.

The growing influence of the Jesuits provoked a strong reaction from the abbey of Port Royal (near Paris). In 1640, shortly before his death, the Bishop of Ypres, Cornelis Jansen, wrote *Augustinus*. In this volume Jansen basically reproduced the theology of Augustine. He insisted that the sinner is free only within the domain of sin. Irresistible grace alone can work good in men. The Jesuits complained about Jansen's book to the pope. In 1653 Innocent X condemned five theses of Jansen:

1. Some commandments of God are impossible for "righteous" men to obey by willing and striving according to the powers that they presently have. They also lack the grace that would make obedience possible.
2. Those in the state of fallen nature never offer resistance to inward grace.
3. To earn merit or demerit in the state of fallen nature, man does not require freedom from necessity. Freedom from coercion is sufficient.
4. Semi-Pelagians rightly admitted the necessity of prevenient inward grace for single acts, even for the beginning of faith. They were heretics because they maintained that this grace is such that the human will can either resist or conform to it.
5. It is semi-Pelagian to say that Christ died, or shed his blood, for all men whatsoever.[20]

Augustinianism was again revived in the church by Pasquier Quesnel. In the eighteenth century he published his *Meditations upon the New Testament.* This work again incited the Jesuits, who succeeded in securing the condemnation of 101 theses of this commentary. "With terrific directness, not only the Augustinian theology, but the entire structure of Augustinian Christianity was here condemned," Seeberg writes. "It is heretical to teach: that the natural man is only sinful; that faith is a gift of God; that grace is given only through faith; that faith is the first grace . . . ; that grace is needed for all good works. . . ."[21]

The Jansenist cause was given a new spark by Blaise Pascal, who wrote a series of essays against the Jesuits. But even the efforts of Pascal did not deter the church's movement away from the course Augustine had established centuries earlier.

Semi-Pelagianism in the Catechism

In the new *Catechism of the Catholic Church* (1994), several articles deal with freedom and human responsibility. Some of these articles include the following:

> Freedom is the power, rooted in reason and will, to act or not to act, to do this or that, and so to perform deliberate actions on one's own responsibility. By free will one shapes one's own life. Human freedom is a force for growth and maturity in truth and goodness; it attains its perfection when directed toward God. . . .
>
> As long as freedom has not bound itself definitively to its ultimate good which is God, there is the possibility of *choosing between good and evil*, and thus of growing in perfection or of failing and sinning. This freedom characterizes properly human acts. It is the basis of praise or blame, merit or reproach.[22]

The words italicized above are italicized in the *Catechism* itself, presumably to stress them. This reveals a semi-Pelagian view whereby fallen man retains the moral ability to choose either good or evil. Elsewhere, the *Catechism* states: "God created man a rational being, conferring on him the dignity of a person who can initiate and control his own actions. 'God willed that man should be "left in the hand of his own counsel," so that he might of his own accord seek his Creator and freely attain his full and blessed perfection by cleaving to him.'"[23]

With respect to original sin, the *Catechism* notes that the church rejected both the Pelagian and the Protestant views. The Reformers, says the *Catechism*, "taught that original sin has radically perverted man and destroyed his freedom; they identified the sin inherited by each man with the tendency to evil *(concupiscentia)*, which would be insurmountable."[24] Unlike both Augustine and the Reformers, Rome does not regard this inclination to evil as insurmountable. It can be overcome by engaging in what the *Catechism* calls "a hard battle."[25] "The whole of man's history has been the story of dour combat with the powers of evil, stretching, so our Lord tells us, from the very dawn of history until the last day. Finding himself in the midst of the battlefield man has to struggle to do what is right, and it is at great cost to himself, and aided by God's grace, that he succeeds in achieving his own inner integrity."[26]

In summary, Rome clearly continues to repudiate pure Pelagianism and to teach that man needs the assistance of divine grace for salvation. Yet Rome also teaches that fallen man retains the capacity (though his will has been weakened) to cooperate with this assisting grace, exercising the will in its natural power. This represents the triumph of semi-Pelagianism over Augustinianism.

Free-will without God's grace
is not free at all,
but is the permanent prisoner
and bondslave of evil,
since it cannot turn itself to good.

Martin Luther

4

We Are in Bondage to Sin:
Martin Luther

On September 1, 1524, Desiderius Erasmus of Rotterdam published his work entitled *Diatribe Concerning Free Will (Diatribe seu collatio de libero arbitrio)*. In December of the following year, Martin Luther responded with his famous *The Bondage of the Will (De servo arbitrio)*. Luther's book was four times longer that Erasmus's and sharply polemical in style.

Luther considered *The Bondage of the Will* to be his most important book, because it spoke to issues that he regarded as being the *cor ecclesiae*, the very heart of the church. In 1537 Luther remarked that none of his books deserved preservation except his children's catechism and *The Bondage of the Will*.[1] B. B. Warfield called *Bondage* the "manifesto" of the Protestant Reformation.[2] Sigurd Normann, Bishop of Oslo, referred to it as "the

finest and most powerful Soli Deo Gloria to be sung in the whole period of the Reformation,"[3] an evaluation quoted approvingly by Gordon Rupp and by J. I. Packer and O. R. Johnston.

Luther begins *The Bondage of the Will* by emphasizing the clarity of Scripture on matters of salvation, and Scripture's role as the final arbiter of the debate. Next he explains how important it is for the Christian to have a correct view of the human will and of the sinner's dependence on God's grace. He chides Erasmus, who had declared that free will involves one of the "useless doctrines that we can do without,"[4] for attaching too little importance to the matters at hand. Luther wrote:

> "It is irreligious, idle and superfluous," you say, "to want to know whether our will effects anything in matters pertaining to eternal salvation, or whether it is wholly passive under the work of grace." But here you speak to the contrary, saying that Christian piety consists in "striving with all our might," and that "apart from the mercy of God our will is ineffective." Here you plainly assert that the will is in some respect active in matters pertaining to eternal salvation, for you represent it as striving; and, again, you represent it as the object of Divine action when you say that without God's mercy it is ineffective. But you do not define the limits within which we should think of the will as acting and as acted upon; you take pains to engender ignorance as to what God's mercy and man's will *can* effect by your very teaching as to what man's will and God's mercy *do* effect![5]

This paragraph captures the essence of the debate between Luther and Erasmus and the classic struggle between Augustinianism and semi-Pelagianism. It focuses on the question of man's moral ability and the degree of his dependence on God's grace. It involves the issue of theocentricity versus anthropocentricity in theology. It touches the issue of the *sola* in *sola gratia*. Both sides affirmed the necessity of grace, but at issue (as in the debate over justification) was the *sola*. It is the question of monergism versus synergism in the initiation of human redemption. Is the decisive factor in salvation something man does or something God does?

It obviously annoyed Luther that Erasmus did not seem to grasp the gravity of the matter. Luther concluded: "So it is not irreligious, idle, or superfluous, but in the highest degree wholesome and necessary, for a Christian to know whether or not his will has anything to do in matters pertaining to salvation."[6]

God's Will and Foreknowledge

Events in the Life of Luther

1483	Born in Eisleben, Germany
1507	Ordained
1512	Became doctor of theology
1517	Posted *Ninety-Five Theses*
1520	Papal bull issued against him
1521	Excommunicated at the Diet of Worms
1525	Married Katherine Von Bora
	Wrote *Bondage of the Will*
1527	Wrote "A Mighty Fortress"
1529	*Large Catechism* and *Small Catechism* published
1534	German Bible published
1546	Died in Eisleben, Germany

For Luther the issue touched heavily on the glory of God. It is a matter of proper knowledge of both self and God. For this reason Luther pressed the issue of the relationship between God's foreknowledge and human events. The question of divine prescience or foreknowledge usually arises in discussions regarding divine providence, predestination, and election. It almost always comes up when free will is discussed. If God foreknows all things that occur and all human actions, do we do all things of necessity? Luther affirms that God does indeed foreknow all contingencies, yet he foreknows nothing contingently.

When speaking of contingencies, we mean *possible actions*. For example, an expert chess player considers the possible moves his opponent may take in response to his own next move. To the chess player these are contingencies, events he cannot predict with certainty. We speak of a contingency plan, to which we will turn if our original plan does not work as hoped. Classic theology affirms that God possesses the attribute of omniscience. This omniscience is related to God's very being as the *ens perfectissimus,* the most perfect being. In his perfection God knows all things perfectly. That is, his perfect omniscience includes a comprehensive knowledge of everything that is.

God knows both the micro- and macro-dimensions of the entire universe. He numbers the very hairs of our heads. Not only does he know what we will do before we do it, but also he knows all the options we could have chosen at the moment. He knows all contingencies. Yet God's knowledge of contingencies is not itself contingent. His foreknowledge is perfect and absolute. He is not a Great Chess Player who must wait to see what we will do, but he knows absolutely what we will do before we do it. Before a word is even formed on our lips, he knows it altogether. Thus Luther responds to Erasmus:

> It is, then, fundamentally necessary and wholesome for Christians to know that God foreknows nothing contingently, but that He foresees, purposes, and does all things according to His own immutable, eternal and infallible will. This bombshell knocks "free-will" flat, and utterly shatters it; so that those who want to assert it must either deny my bombshell, or pretend not to notice it, or find some other way of dodging it. . . .
>
> . . . You insist that we should learn the immutability of God's will, while forbidding us to know the immutability of His foreknowledge! Do you suppose that He does not will what He foreknows, or that He does not foreknow what He wills? If He wills what He foreknows, His will is eternal and changeless, because His nature is so. From which it follows, by resistless logic, that all we do, however it may appear to us to be done mutably and contingently, is in reality done necessarily and immutably in respect of God's will. For the will of God is effective and cannot be impeded, since power belongs to God's nature; and His wisdom is such that He cannot be deceived. Since then His will is not impeded, what is done cannot but be done where, when, how, as far as, and by whom, He foresees and wills.[7]

Luther forces attention to the nature and character of God. Luther's crucial point is that God wills what he foreknows and foreknows whatever he wills. Luther speaks here of "resistless logic." This does not mean that people cannot or do not resist these assertions. Church history is filled with the record of such resistance. His point is that this resistance cannot destroy the argument. If God wills that something should come to pass, he cannot be ignorant of it. He cannot will without knowing what he is willing. Most thinkers will readily agree to this part of the equation. It is the first assertion that has evoked furious debate: God wills whatsoever he foreknows. Augustine made the same assertion, but with a qualifier: God ordains (in a certain sense) everything that comes to pass.

Augustine's "in a certain sense" softens the blow a bit. Behind the assertions of Augustine and Luther lies the full doctrine of God. Both rigorously affirmed his omnipotence as well as his immutability and omniscience. Omnipotence contains the idea that God has all power and authority over his creation, including the actions of human beings. Whatever God knows will happen, he knows he can prevent from happening. Even if God's will is regarded as passive or is described as his "permissive will," he still has the power and authority to prevent it. If, for example, God knows I will choose to sin, he has the power to annihilate me in an instant to keep me from sinning. If he chooses not to destroy me but to "let" me sin, he chooses to do so. Insofar as he knows it and permits it, it is within the scope of his will that I do it.

Necessity without Compulsion

If God knows in advance what will happen, then what happens is certain to take place. God's foreknowledge is not uncertain. This raises the specter of *necessity:* if it is certain from eternity that something will take place, is this event *necessary?* And if so, how can there be any contingencies, or how can man possess any free moral agency?

Luther was uncomfortable with the term *necessity.* "I could wish, indeed, that a better term was available for our discussion than the accepted one, *necessity,* which cannot accurately be used of either man's will or God's," Luther says. "Its meaning is too harsh, and foreign to the subject; for it suggests some sort of compulsion, and something that is against one's will, which is no part of the view under debate. The will, whether it be God's or man's, does what it does, good or bad, under no compulsion, but just as it wants or pleases, as if totally free."[8]

Luther did affirm that God necessitates all things, but only in the sense that his will makes them certain. Luther regarded this point as vital to the whole of Christianity. "For if you hesitate to believe, or are too proud to acknowledge, that God foreknows and wills all things, not contingently, but necessarily and immutably, how can you believe, trust and rely on His promises?" Luther asserts. "If, then, we are taught and believe that we ought to be ignorant of the necessary foreknowledge of God and the necessity of events, Christian faith is utterly destroyed, and the promises of God and the whole gospel fall to the ground completely; for the Christian's chief and only comfort in every adversity lies in knowing that God does not lie, but brings all things to pass immutably, and that His will cannot be resisted, altered or impeded."[9]

Here Luther's chief pastoral concern in the theological debate becomes clear: the believer's comfort and hope. To trust in the promises of God is to trust in his perfect power and integrity— that he will bring to pass what he has promised to bring to pass. The Christian's joy is to know that God's promises will come to pass of necessity.

So, despite his hesitancy over the danger and inadequacy of the word *necessity,* Luther uses it. But he does so with the qualification that necessity does not mean compulsion. The grand mystery of providence is that God brings his will to pass through and by the real choices of moral agents. His own actions are not compelled by external forces, nor does he compel humans to do his will. He brings his will to pass through the means and agency of his creatures and their uncompelled and noncoerced choices.

Erasmus contended that such arcane truths should not be proclaimed. "What can be more useless than to publish to the world the paradox that all we do is done, not by 'free-will,' but of mere necessity, and Augustine's view that God works in us both good and evil; that He rewards His own good works in us, and punishes His own evil works in us?" wrote Erasmus in the preface to *The Diatribe.* "What a flood-gate of iniquity would the spread of such news open to people! What wicked man would amend his life? Who would believe that God loved him? Who would fight against his flesh?"[10]

The concerns mentioned by Erasmus were precisely the same as those of the semi-Pelagians who disputed Augustine. It was also a pastoral concern, but different from Luther's. The danger of fatalism, which would render all human action an exercise in futility, was a grave concern for Erasmus. Luther responds by first quoting Erasmus, then answering him.

Related Works by Luther
The Bondage of the Will. Translated by J. I. Packer and O. R. Johnston. Cambridge: James Clarke / Westwood, N.J.: Revell, 1957.
Luther and Erasmus: Free Will and Salvation. Edited by E. Gordon Rupp and Philip S. Watson. The Library of Christian Classics, vol. 17. Philadelphia: Westminster, 1969.
Martin Luther's Basic Theological Writings. Edited by Timothy F. Lull. Minneapolis: Fortress, 1989.

Erasmus: Who will try and reform his life?

Luther: Nobody!

Erasmus: Who will believe that God loves him?

Luther: Nobody! Nobody can! But the elect shall believe it; and the rest shall perish without believing it, raging and blaspheming.

Erasmus: A flood-gate of iniquity is opened by our doctrines.

Luther: So be it.[11]

Luther insisted that, far from opening this flood-gate, he was merely being faithful to the word of God. It is God who publishes these things, and he does so for the sake of his elect.

Thereafter Luther returns to the question of necessity:

> I said "of necessity"; I did not say "of compulsion"; I meant, by a necessity, not of *compulsion,* but of what they call *immutability*. That is to say: a man without the Spirit of God does not do evil against his will, under pressure, as though he were taken by the scruff of the neck and dragged into it, like a thief . . . being dragged off against his will to punishment; but he does it spontaneously and voluntarily. And this willingness or volition is

something which he cannot in his own strength eliminate, restrain or alter. . . . the will cannot change itself, nor give itself another bent. . . .

On the other hand: when God works in us, the will is changed under the sweet influence of the Spirit of God. Once more it desires and acts, not of compulsion, but of its own desire and spontaneous inclination. . . .[12]

The position of Augustine, Martin Luther, John Calvin, and others is so often caricatured to mean that in God's gracious election he brings people kicking and screaming against their wills into his kingdom. The Augustinian view is that God changes the recalcitrant and enslaved sinner's will by the Spirit's changing his internal bent, disposition, or inclination. Augustinians have spelled out this view so often and so clearly, it is amazing that the caricature is so often repeated.

In *The Diatribe* Erasmus argued that a will that is powerless without grace is not really free. Luther gives this reply: "You describe the power of 'free-will' as small, and wholly ineffective apart from the grace of God. Agreed? Now then, I ask you: if God's grace is wanting, if it is taken away from that small power, what can it do? It is ineffective, you say, and can do nothing good. So it will not do what God or His grace wills. Why? Because we have now taken God's grace away from it, and what the grace of God does not do is not good. Hence it follows that 'free-will' without God's grace is not free at all, but is the permanent prisoner and bondslave of evil, since it cannot turn itself to good."[13]

Luther was concerned that the phrase *free will* is profoundly misleading to most people. Its common meaning is "a human ability to turn freely in any direction, to either the good or the bad." Luther called the phrase *free will* "too grandiose and comprehensive and fulsome."[14] He concludes that "this false idea of 'free-will' is a real threat to salvation, and a delusion fraught with the most perilous consequences."[15]

The Meaning of Free Will

After responding to Erasmus's arguments based on appeals to ancient writers and to his assertion that the Bible is not clear about these matters, Luther turns to the main body of Erasmus's work. Luther deals first with Erasmus's definition of *free will:* "a power of the human will by which a man may apply himself to those things that lead to eternal salvation, or turn away from the same."[16]

Luther then produces his own understanding of what Erasmus means by *free will:*

> I suppose, then, that this "power of the human will" means a power, or faculty, or disposition, or aptitude to will or not to will, to choose or reject, to approve or disapprove, and to perform all the other actions of the will. Now, what it means for this same power to "apply itself" or to "turn away" I do not see, unless this refers to the actual willing or not willing, choosing or rejecting, approving or disapproving—that is, the very action of the will itself. So we must suppose that this power is something that comes between the will and its action, something by which the will itself elicits the act of willing or not willing, and by means of which the action of willing or not willing is elicited. Nothing else is imaginable or conceivable.[17]

Luther sees in Erasmus's view a reversion to the view of Pelagius, though with less sophistication. He decries Erasmus's understanding of past philosophical debates on this issue. He then discusses Erasmus's three distinct views of free will: "Out of one view about 'free-will' you devise three! The first, that of those who deny that man can will good without special grace, neither start, nor make progress, nor finish, etc. seems to you 'severe, but probable enough.'. . . The second, that of those who contend that 'free-will' avails for nothing but sinning, and that grace alone works good in us, etc., seems to you 'more severe'; and the third, that of those who say that 'free-will' is an empty term, and God works in us both good and evil, and all that comes to pass is of mere necessity, seems to you, 'most severe.' It is against these two last that you profess to be writing."[18]

Luther asserts that the three different views enumerated by Erasmus make distinctions where there are no differences. All three refer to the same, but with different words. Luther asks how Erasmus can call the first view "probable enough" when it is clearly at odds with Erasmus's own definition? "You said," writes Luther, "that 'free-will' is a power of the human will by which a man can apply himself to good; but here you say, and approve of its being said, that man without grace cannot will good."[19]

Luther says: "The definition affirms what the statement parallel to it denies! So there is found in your 'free-will' at the same moment a *yes* and a *no,* and in the same breath you say that we are both right and wrong, and that you yourself are both right and wrong, over one and the same doctrine and article! Do you think that to apply itself to what bears on eternal salvation (as your definition says that 'free-will' does) is not *good?* If there were enough good in free-will for it to apply itself to good, it would have no need of grace! So the 'free-will' you define is one thing, and the free-will you defend is another."[20]

At this point Luther indicates that Erasmus's definition of free will does not require grace to turn to the good or to God. If grace is not required but merely assists man, then Erasmus's definition of *free will* is not essentially different from Pelagius's. But Luther noted that the free will Erasmus defined was not the free will he was defending. Erasmus did not set out to defend a pure Pelagian view of free will. Elsewhere in *The Diatribe,* Erasmus declared that "the human will after sin is so depraved that it has lost its freedom and is forced to serve sin, and cannot recall itself to a better state."[21]

If this is the view Erasmus is defending, Luther argues, then Erasmus is really conceding something to Luther's own view: "If, now, 'free-will' without grace has lost its freedom, is forced to serve sin, and cannot will good, I should like to know what that effort and endeavour amount to which the first view, the 'probable' one, leaves it. It cannot be a good effort or endeavour, for 'free-will' cannot will good, as the view states and you grant."[22]

This is the classic argument *reductio ad absurdum.* Luther argues "to the man," assuming his opponent's own premises and carrying them to their logical conclusion. He calls Erasmus's view a freaky kind of paradox by which Erasmus finally affirms the very thing he set out to deny or denies the very thing he set out to affirm. Luther says the entire *Diatribe* is "nothing but a noble act of 'free-will' condemning itself in its own defense, and defending itself by its own condemnation."

Luther then compares this view with the two others Erasmus had delineated:

> . . . The second is the 'more severe' one, which holds that 'free-will' avails for nothing but sin. This is certainly Augustine's opinion, which he expresses in many places, particularly in his book *Of the Spirit and the Letter* [3.5], where he uses those very words. The third is the 'most severe' view, that of Wycliffe and Luther: that *free-will* is an empty term. . . .
>
> . . . I call God [as my] witness that by the words of the last two views I meant to say nothing, and wished nothing to be understood, but what is stated in the first view. Nor do I think that Augustine intended anything but this, nor do I understand any other meaning from his words than what the first view affirms. So . . . the three views retailed by the *Diatribe* are to my mind nothing but the one view which I hold. For once it is granted and settled that 'free-will' has lost its freedom, and is bound in the service of sin, and can will no good. I can gather nothing from these words but that *free-will* is an empty term whose reality is lost. A lost freedom, to my way of speaking, is no freedom at all, and to give the name of freedom to something that has no freedom is to apply to it a term that is empty of meaning. . . .[23]

Related Works about Luther

Bainton, Roland H. *Here I Stand: A Life of Martin Luther.* New York: New American Library, 1955.

Horton, Michael S. "Martin Luther, *Bondage of the Will.* " In *Tabletalk* 17 (January 1993): 13–14, 17.

McGrath, Alister. *Luther's Theology of the Cross.* Oxford and Cambridge, Mass.: Blackwell, 1985.

Martin Luther: The Early Years. In *Christian History* 11, 2 (1992).

Martin Luther: The Later Years. In *Christian History* 12, 3 (1993).

Packer, J. I., and O. R. Johnston. "Historical and Theological Introduction." In Martin Luther. *The Bondage of the Will.* Cambridge: James Clarke / Westwood, N.J.: Revell, 1957.

Rupp, Gordon. *Luther's Progress to the Diet of Worms.* New York: Harper and Row, 1964.

"If Thou Art Willing . . ."

Next Luther responds to another objection Erasmus had raised, based on biblical texts that seem to imply that man can perform anything God commands. This issue is similar to the one that provoked Pelagius's initial reaction against the prayer of Augustine, in which he asked God to grant what he commanded. In *The Diatribe* Erasmus appeals to one of the Apocryphal books: "Ecclesiasticus, by saying 'if thou art willing to keep,' indicates that there is a will in man to keep or not to keep; otherwise, what is the sense of saying to him who has no will, 'if thou wilt'? Is it not ridiculous to say to a blind man: 'if thou art willing to see, thou wilt find a treasure'? or to a deaf man: 'if thou art willing to hear, I will tell thee a good story'? That would be mocking their misery."[24]

This issue raises a question about the very integrity of God. If he commands something to be done that cannot in fact be done, then this command seems to be cruel and unjust. This would, as Erasmus says, mock human misery. He infers that a divine commandment implies an ability to obey. Otherwise the creature cannot be held morally responsible for the action. The very word *responsibility* bespeaks the ability to respond.

Luther responds by chiding human reason for making unwise inferences. What he elsewhere calls the "evangelical usage of the law," Luther here describes as a divine strategy for showing his morally impotent creatures their very impotence:

> If, now, God, as a Father, deals with us as with His sons, with a view to showing us the impotence of which we are ignorant; or as a faithful physician, with a view to making known to us our disease; or if, to taunt His enemies, who proudly resist His counsel and the laws He has set forth (by which He achieves this end most effectively), He should say: "do," "hear," "keep," or: "if thou shalt hear," "if thou art willing," "if thou shalt do"; can it be fairly concluded from this that therefore we can do these things freely, or else God is mocking us? Why should not this conclusion follow rather: therefore, God is trying us, that by His law He may bring us to a knowledge of our impotence. . . . [25]

Here Luther demonstrates the difference between a *possible inference* and a *necessary inference*. When God does something his purpose for which we do not know, we are left to speculate regarding his purpose. Erasmus infers that if man is powerless to do what God commands, then God's reason for the command is to mock human misery. Such is a *possible inference,* but it quickly vanishes when we bring into consideration the character of God. More importantly, Erasmus infers from the command that we are able to obey it. This is also, according to Luther, a *possible inference,* not a *necessary inference.* To make this point, Luther argues much like Paul when the apostle says the law is a schoolmaster to drive us to Christ. We are commanded to obey the entire law, to be perfect. This does not mean (unless we embrace unadulterated Pelagianism) that we are morally capable of achieving perfection.

According to the laws of immediate inference, one can infer from the statement "If you are willing . . ." nothing about who has the power so to will. This is a condition statement, indicated by the presence of the word *if.* It is like the formula, If A, then B. If the condition is met (A), then the conclusion will follow (B). This formula merely indicates a connection between A and B.

A text frequently mentioned in this regard is John 3:16, which promises that whosoever believes will not perish. The text explicitly teaches that if someone does A (believes), then he will not have B (perishing) and will have C (eternal life). The text says nothing about who will believe or who can believe. It may imply that some can or will believe, but an implication cannot annul an explicit statement.

This is where the debate will proceed. Luther will endeavor to show that the Scriptures explicitly deny man's moral ability to do what God commands. He will apply the principle of interpretation that the implicit is to be interpreted in light of the explicit, not the explicit in light of the implicit.

Erasmus continues to appeal to texts that impose obligation on the sinner, arguing that such obligation necessitates moral ability: "If it is not in the power of every man to keep what is commanded, all the exhortations in the Scriptures, and all the promises, threats, expostulations, reproofs, adjurations, blessings, curses and hosts of precepts, are of necessity useless."[26]

Luther sees this conclusion as gratuitous, involving a quantum leap of logic. Again the possible inference is elevated to the level of a necessary inference. Without plenary ability to perform what is commanded, the commands would be necessarily useless. Luther replies:

> The *Diatribe* is continually forgetting the question at issue, and dealing with matters foreign to its purpose; and it does not see that all these things make [a case] more strongly against itself than against us. From all these passages it proves freedom and ability to fulfil all things, as the very words of the inference which it draws declare; whereas, its intention was to establish "such a 'free-will' as can will no good without grace, and an endeavour that may not be ascribed to one's own strength." ...
>
> ... and now let the *Diatribe* itself recant its own words, where it said that 'free-will' can will no good without grace! Let it now say that 'free-will' has such power that it not only wills good, but keeps the greatest commandments, yes, all the commandments, with ease![27]

Here Luther is driving Erasmus where Erasmus does not want to go, straight into the arms of Pelagius. If Erasmus's argument is sound, then it proves too much, namely, plenary ability without the assistance of grace. Luther concludes: "Thus, nothing is less proved by the whole of this discursive, repetitive and laboured discussion than that which had to be proved, that is, the 'probable view' which describes 'free-will' as 'so impotent that it cannot will any good without grace, but is forced into the service of sin; though it has endeavour, which yet may not be ascribed to its own strength.' A real freak!—it can do nothing in its own strength, and yet it has endeavour within its own strength; its constitution involves a very obvious contradiction."[28]

"To Them Gave He Power ... "

Next Erasmus cites the words from John 1 "to them gave he power to become the sons of God" (John 1:12 KJV), saying, "How is power given [to] them to become the sons of God, if there is no freedom of our will?"[29]

Luther replies: "This passage also is a hammer against 'free-will,' as is almost the whole of John's gospel; yet it too is cited in favour of 'free-will'! Let us look at it, please! John is not speaking of any work of man, great or small, but of the actual renewal and transformation of the old man, who is a son of the devil, into the new man, who is a son of God. In this, man is simply *passive* (as the term is used); he *does* nothing, but the whole of him *becomes* something. John is speaking of this becoming: He says that we become the sons of God, by a power divinely given us—not by any power of 'free-will' inherent in us!"[30]

Later Luther discusses God's role in hardening Pharaoh's heart. Luther explains this difficult concept from the Old Testament by saying: "Thus God hardens Pharaoh: He presents to the ungodly, evil will of Pharaoh His own word and work, which Pharaoh's will hates, by reason of its own inbred fault and natural corruption. God does not alter that will within by His Spirit, but goes on presenting and bringing pressure to bear; and Pharaoh, having in mind his own strength, wealth and power, trusts to them by this same fault of his nature. . . . As soon as God presents to it from without something that naturally irritates and offends it, Pharaoh cannot escape being hardened. . . ."[31]

Pharaoh's heart is hardened by necessity, but not because God created fresh evil within it or because God coerced Pharaoh to sin. Rather the hardening was the natural result of Pharaoh's internal corruption as it met up with God's persistent will and command.

Does the necessity of the result (Pharaoh's heart being hardened) mean that compulsion was involved? If God willed that Pharaoh's heart be hardened, then that hardening would of necessity come to pass. If it comes to pass by necessity, how can it do so without compulsion? *The Diatribe* allows for both necessity and free will. "Not all necessity excludes 'free-will,'" Erasmus said. "Thus, God the Father begets a Son of necessity; yet He begets Him willingly and freely, for He is not forced to do so."[32]

"Are we now discussing compulsion and force?" Luther responds. "Have I not put on record in many books that I am talking about *necessity of immutability?* I know that the Father begets willingly, and that Judas betrayed Christ willingly. . . . I distinguish two necessities: one I call necessity of force *(necessitatem violentam),* referring to action; the other I call necessity of infallibility *(necessitatem infallibilem),* referring to time."[33]

After duels over several Old Testament texts, the debate moves to the New Testament. Erasmus objects to Luther's appeal to Jesus' statement, "Without Me you can do nothing" (John 15:5 NKJV). Luther responds: "It catches hold of this little word *nothing,* cuts its throat with many words and examples, and by means of a 'convenient explanation' brings it to this: that *nothing* may mean the same as 'a little imperfect something.'"[34]

Erasmus had interpreted this text in elliptical fashion, according to which it means that without Christ the sinner can do nothing *perfectly.* This really exercises Luther's wrath. He says, "Unless you prove that 'nothing' in this passage not only *may,* but *must* be taken to mean 'a little something,' you have done nothing with your vast profusion of words and examples but fight fire with dry straw!"[35] Later he adds, "It is utterly unheard-of grammar and logic to say that *nothing* is the same as *something;* to logicians, the thing is an impossibility, for the two are contradictory!"[36]

After responding to Erasmus's proof texts for his position, Luther concludes his book by presenting an exegetical case for his own position.

When the will is enchained as the slave of sin, it cannot make a movement towards goodness, far less steadily pursue it.

John Calvin

5

We Are Voluntary Slaves: *John Calvin*

*T*he modern controversy over free will is so frequently linked to John Calvin and "Calvinism" that many assume the Swiss Reformer was singularly responsible for ascribing to fallen man an enslaved will. The debate over free will is usually related to Calvin's idea of predestination.

In reality there is little if anything novel in Calvin's view of either the will or predestination. Martin Luther wrote more extensively than Calvin on both of these subjects, and Calvin's work on them may be considered nothing more than a footnote to Luther's. Both Reformers relied heavily on the seminal thought of Augustine on these matters. Perhaps Calvin's name figures so prominently in the modern discussion of the will because his followers in Reformed churches have done so much to keep the Augustinian tradition alive.

Calvin did, however, address the question of free will, and his place in the history of theology requires us to summarize his teaching on the question. He devotes a few chapters in his *Institutes of the Christian Religion* to the question of free will.

Calvin begins his treatment of the will by establishing the course of his inquiry. He seeks to avoid two errors. The first is that of ignoring the subject altogether: "Man being devoid of all uprightness, immediately takes occasion from the fact to indulge in sloth, and having no ability in himself for the study of righteousness, treats the whole subject as if he had no concern in it."[1]

The second error to avoid is the failure to give proper honor to God in effecting our redemption. To err in our understanding of the fallen will is to run the risk of debasing the glory of God.

> On the other hand, man cannot arrogate anything, however minute, to himself, without robbing God of his honour, and through rash confidence subjecting himself to a fall. To keep free of both these rocks, our proper course will be, first, to show that man has no remaining good in himself, and is beset on every side by the most miserable destitution; and then teach him to aspire to the goodness of which he is devoid, and the liberty of which he has been deprived. . . . What remains, therefore, now that man is stripped of all his glory, [but] to acknowledge the God for whose kindness he failed to be grateful, when he was loaded with the riches of his grace? Not having glorified him by the acknowledgment of his blessings, now, at least, he ought to glorify him by the confession of his poverty.[2]

Pagan and Christian Views

Calvin briefly surveys theories of the will held by pagan philosophers. They commonly distinguished the faculties of the mind (the seat of reason), the senses (the link to physical responses), and the will. The mind is the superior faculty, by which virtue is achieved. The senses are the inferior power and are usually responsible for leading the mind into error and delusion. The will occupies an intermediate place between reason and sense, and it possesses the power and freedom to follow the good inclinations of the mind or to surrender to the baser appetites of the senses.

Citing Cicero, Calvin says: "Hence Cicero says, in the person of Cotta, that as every one acquires virtue for himself, no wise man ever thanked the gods for it. 'We are praised,' says he, 'for virtue, and glory in virtue, but this could not be, if virtue were the gift of God, and not from ourselves.' A little after [this], he

Events in the Life of Calvin	
1509	Born in Noyon, Picardy, France
1533	Converted
1536	Published *Institutes* (1st ed.)
1536	Moved to Geneva
1538	Accepted a call from a Strasbourg church
1540	Married Idelette de Bure
1541	Moved back to Geneva
1559	Published *Institutes* (last Latin ed.)
1564	Died in Geneva

adds, 'The opinion of all mankind is, that fortune must be sought from God, wisdom from ourselves.'"[3]

Calvin says secular philosophy almost universally considers human reason to be sufficient for virtuous living. Then he notes the views espoused by Christian philosophers and theologians, who acknowledge that man is fallen to the degree that even sound reason is seriously injured. But he then maintains that the views of many, if not most, Christian thinkers come too close to those of secular philosophers. He speculates that a chief cause for this is the reluctance of theologians to stray too far from philosophical opinion, to teach "anything which the majority of mankind might deem absurd." So they seek, "in some measure, to reconcile the doctrine of Scripture with the dogmas of philosophy."[4]

Calvin's speculation at this point should give us pause. We live in an era in which secular thought and humanistic philosophy are so dominant that Christians often accept uncritically the humanist view of human freedom.

Calvin shows how this occurred in church history. He cites some of the fathers of the early church: "Chrysostom says, 'God having placed good and evil in our power, has given us full freedom of choice; he does not keep back the unwilling, but embraces the willing.' . . . 'As the whole is not done by divine assistance, we ourselves must of necessity bring [something].' . . . 'Let us bring what is our own, God will supply the rest.' In unison with this, Jerome says, 'It is ours to begin, God's to finish.'"[5]

Calvin sees confusion in many of the ancient fathers on the subject of the will: "Persons professing to be the disciples of Christ have spoken too much like the philosophers on this subject. As if human nature were still in its integrity, the term *free will* has always been in use amid the Latins, while the Greeks were not ashamed to use a still more presumptuous term—viz. *autexousion*—as if man had still full power in himself."[6]

Calvin summarizes the view of the will that emerged among the Scholastics, paying particular attention to that of Peter Lombard: "The schools . . . [enumerate] three kinds of freedom: the first, a freedom from necessity; the second, a freedom from sin; and the third, a freedom from misery: the first naturally so inherent in man, that he cannot possibly be deprived of it; while through sin the other two have been lost. I willingly admit this distinction, except in so far as it confounds *necessity* with *compulsion*."[7]

Calvin agrees with Lombard, with the proviso that necessity and compulsion must not be confused. At this point Calvin echoes the sentiments of Luther over against Erasmus. Here freedom simply means that man still has the ability to act voluntarily, without compulsion, which Calvin readily admits. He says: "This is perfectly true: but why should so small a matter have been dignified with so proud a title? An admirable freedom! that man is not forced to be the servant of sin, while he is, however, *ethelodoulos* (a voluntary slave); his will being bound by the fetters of sin. . . . If any one, then, chooses to make use of this term, without attaching any bad meaning to it, he shall not be troubled by me on that account; but as it cannot be retained without very great danger, I think the abolition of it would be of great advantage to the Church. I am unwilling to use it myself; and others, if they will take my advice, will do well to abstain from it."[8]

Calvin then reiterates the importance of guarding the glory of God. We must not boast of power within ourselves to do for ourselves what God alone can do for us. To bask in our own power to incline ourselves to the things of God is to mirror and reflect the sin of Adam and Eve. It is to be seduced by the serpent's promise that we will be like gods.

With help from Augustine, Calvin gives a ringing call to proper humility. An orator was once asked, according to Augustine, "What is the first precept in eloquence?"

"Delivery," the orator answered.

"What is the second?"

"Delivery."

"What [is] the third?"

"Delivery."

"So," Augustine concluded, "if you ask me in regard to the precepts of the Christian Religion, I will answer, first, second, and third, 'Humility.'"[9]

Effects of the Fall

Calvin next draws a parallel between the state of the mind and the state of the will. The natural faculty of reason remains intact after the fall, but the *soundness* of our thinking has been darkened by sin. Man is presently in exile from the kingdom of God, and only the grace of regeneration can restore him. Though man's power of rational thinking has not been utterly destroyed and he has not become a mere brute, the light of his reason is so smothered by darkness that it cannot shine forth to any good effect.

Man can still gain valuable knowledge with respect to what Calvin calls inferior objects. Calvin distinguishes an intelligence concerning earthly things from an intelligence concerning heavenly things. The former includes the knowledge of art, mechanics, economics, and so forth. He even (like Augustine) commends learning in certain areas from pagan thinkers: "Therefore, in reading profane authors, the admirable light of truth displayed in them should remind us, that the human mind, however much fallen and perverted from its original integrity, is still adorned and invested with admirable gifts from its Creator."[10]

Calvin regarded reason as an essential property of human nature. The fall did not obliterate man's natural humanity. Man still has the capacity to think, but this capacity has been severely damaged by sin. This is true particularly with respect to spiritual things. In our understanding of the things of God, Calvin says we are "blinder than moles."[11] For our knowledge of heavenly things we must depend on God's gracious illumination. The understanding required for a person to enter the kingdom of God comes from the Holy Spirit alone.

What power remains in the human will after the fall? Calvin argues that man does not rationally choose or pursue what is good. Man has a desire for good things (we all want to be happy, for example), but apart from the Spirit we do not aspire to the good that is a prerequisite for eternal felicity.

Man's fallen and corrupt nature is described in the New Testament as "flesh." Calvin points to Jesus' words to Nicodemus: to enter the kingdom, one must first be reborn (John 3:3). Regeneration is necessary because the only thing the flesh can beget is flesh.

Calvin says: "Grant that there is nothing in human nature but flesh, and then extract something good out of it if you can. But it will be said, that the word *flesh* applies only to the sensual, and not to the higher part of the soul. This, however, is completely refuted by the words both of Christ and [of] his apostle. The statement of our Lord is, that a man must be born again, because he is flesh. He requires not to be born again, with reference to the body. But a mind is not born again merely by having some portion of it reformed. It must be totally renewed. . . . But we have nothing of the Spirit except through regeneration."[12]

Here Calvin gets to the heart of the matter. Regeneration is a requirement for a person to be liberated from bondage to sin. Just as the mind cannot discern spiritual things without the prior illumination of the Holy Spirit, so the flesh will not incline itself to God without first receiving the grace of regeneration. Like Luther and Augustine, Calvin sees the necessity of a divine initiative to free man from his moral bondage. He cannot free himself by exerting his fleshy will.

When the will is enchained as the slave of sin, it cannot make a movement towards goodness, far less steadily pursue it. Every such movement is the first step in that conversion to God, which in Scripture is entirely ascribed to divine grace. . . . Nevertheless, there remains a will which both inclines and hastens on with the strongest affection towards sin; man, when placed under this bondage, [was] deprived not of will, but of soundness of will. . . . Moreover, when I say that the will, deprived of liberty, is led or dragged by necessity to evil, it is strange that any should deem the expression harsh, seeing there is no absurdity in it, and it is not at variance with pious use. It does, however, offend those who know not how to distinguish between necessity and compulsion.[13]

Related Works by Calvin

The Bondage and Liberation of the Will: A Defence of the Orthodox Doctrine of Human Choice against Pighius. Edited by A. N. S. Lane. Translated by G. I. Davies. Grand Rapids: Baker / Carlisle, Cumbria: Paternoster, 1996.

Institutes of the Christian Religion. 2 vols. Translated by Henry Beveridge. 1845. Reprint. Grand Rapids: Eerdmans, 1964. Book 2, chapters 2–3.

The Institutes of Christian Religion. Edited by Tony Lane and Hilary Osborne. London: Hodder & Stoughton, 1986 / Grand Rapids: Baker, 1987. Pages 85–102.

Calvin asks the rhetorical question, Is not God necessarily good? God can do nothing but good. This is not because God is subject to compulsion, but because he acts altogether according to his own perfect nature. Since it is "necessary" for God to be good, can we say that therefore he is not free or has no will? Likewise, man sins of necessity and he sins willfully.

"Let this, then, be regarded as the sum of the distinction," Calvin writes. "Man, since he was corrupted by the fall, sins not forced or unwillingly, but voluntarily, by a most forward bias of the mind; not by violent compulsion, or external force, but by the movement of his own passion; and yet such is the depravity of his nature, that he cannot move and act except in the direction of evil. If this is true, the thing not obscurely expressed is, that he is under a necessity of sinning."[14]

Calvin pleads that his doctrine is not new, but merely echoes the position of Augustine. Then he turns his attention from the malady to the remedy, God's liberation of the sinner from his bondage. Calvin cites Paul's letter to the Philippians, where the apostle speaks of God's having "begun" a good work within us

(Phil. 1:6). Calvin interprets this to mean the initiation of conversion in the will. The work of the Spirit in the will is what initiates conversion to Christ. Calvin explains: "God, therefore, begins the good work in us by exciting in our hearts a desire, a love, and a study of righteousness, or (to speak more correctly) by turning, training, and guiding our hearts unto righteousness. . . . I say the will is abolished, but not in so far as it is [a] will, for in conversion everything essential to our original nature remains: I also say, that it is created anew, not because the will then begins to exist, but because it is turned from evil to good."[15]

Clearly Calvin does not mean to teach that in conversion the will is destroyed. Rather it is changed in its orientation or disposition. He uses the word *turn*. The will's direction is changed. Whereas the unconverted will is directed only toward evil, the regenerated will is now directed toward God.

When God turns a person's will, he who was formerly unwilling to turn to God and was indisposed to spiritual things, becomes willing to come to God. This change in the will's direction is accomplished by God's regenerating grace. This raises the question of the irresistible character of regenerating grace. The caricature of Augustinian doctrine is that God forces unwilling people to come to him. In place of this the semi-Pelagian says man has the capacity to cooperate with regenerating grace or reject it.

Chrysostom had argued that "whom he draws, he draws willingly."[16] His notion in itself is not incorrect, but Calvin is uncomfortable with what Chrysostom insinuates: "that the Lord only stretches out his hand, and waits to see whether we will be pleased to take his aid." "We grant that, as man was originally constituted, he could incline to either side," Calvin continues, "but since he has taught us by his example how miserable a thing free will is if God works not in us to will and to do, of what use to us were grace imparted in such scanty measure? . . . The Apostle's doctrine is not, that the grace of a good will is offered to us if we will accept . . . it, but that God himself is pleased so to work in us as to guide, turn, and govern our heart by his Spirit, and reign in it as his own possession."[17]

Here Calvin clearly comes down on the side of monergism. The work of regenerating grace is not a mere external offer, but an internal re-creation by God, which effects what he intends to effect. A mere external offer of grace or assistance to the weakened will, which Calvin calls a "scanty" kind of grace, is insufficient to bring the sinner to faith and salvation. An external offer does nothing to overcome the flesh's bondage to sin, but, in a sense would only mock it. The flesh is so impotent that more than an external drawing is needed to liberate the creature from his bondage. The heart of stone must be changed by God into a heart of flesh.

We must be careful not to confuse two different usages of the word *flesh* in the Bible. The dominant New Testament meaning of *flesh* is the sinner's fallen and corrupt nature, which avails nothing toward righteousness or spiritual vitality. Here *flesh* is the opposite of *spirit.*

In the Old Testament phrase "the heart of flesh," *flesh* is the opposite of *stone.* Man is in moral bondage because his heart is recalcitrant, ossified. Stones do not willingly embrace the things of God. When it says God will change the heart of stone into a heart of flesh, it means, not that he will make it evil, but that he will make it a living, pulsating force that is alive to him and his kingdom. In this usage, the heart of flesh is a regenerated heart. In the other usage, the heart of flesh is an unregenerated heart.

Calvin says:

Therefore, to meet the infirmity of the human will, and prevent it from failing, how weak soever it might be, divine grace was made to act on it inseparably and uninterruptedly. Augustine next entering fully into the question, how our hearts follow the movement when God affects them, necessarily says, indeed, that the Lord draws men by their own wills; wills, however, which he himself has produced. We have now an attestation by Augustine to the truth which we are specially desirous to maintain—viz. that the grace offered by the Lord is not merely one which every individual has full liberty of choosing to receive or reject, but a grace which produces in the heart both choice and will: so that all the good works which follow after are its fruit and effect; the only will which yields obedience being the will which grace itself has made.[18]

Answers to Paris Professors

In 1542 the theological faculty of the University of Arles drew up a list of 25 articles setting forth the tenets of Roman Catholic orthodoxy. These articles were to be binding on students and faculty alike. Calvin penned a response to these articles, point by point. What interests us at this point is article 2, "Of Free Will": "... in man there is a free will with which he can do good or evil, and by means of which, were he even in mortal sin, he is able, with the help of God, to rise again to grace."[19]

It is significant that this article mentions both the power of the will to rise again to grace and the need of God's help. The will, with divine help, rises to grace. The will is free, able to do good or evil.

To this article Calvin offers the following "antidote":

Since the Spirit of God declares that every imagination of man's heart from infancy is evil (Gen. 6:5; 8:21); that there is none righteous, none that understandeth, none that seeketh after God (Ps. 14:3); but that all are useless, corrupt, void of the fear of God, full of fraud, bitterness, and all kinds of iniquity, and have fallen short of the glory of God (Rom. 3:10); since he proclaims that the carnal mind is enmity against God, and does not even leave us the power of thinking a good thought (Rom. 8:6; 2 Cor. 3:5), we maintain with Augustine, that man, by making a bad use of free will, lost both himself and it. Again, that the will being overcome by the corruption into which it fell, nature has no liberty. Again, that no will is free which is subject to lusts which conquer and enchain it.[20]

After summarizing key biblical texts and quoting from Augustine, Calvin speaks of the sinner's total dependence on divine grace to recover his liberty to do good:

In like manner, since God declares that it is his own work to renew the heart, out of stone to make it flesh, to write his law on the heart, and put it in the inward parts, to make us ... walk in his precepts, to give both good will and the result of it, to put the fear of his name into our hearts, that we may never withdraw from it ... we again conclude with Augustine, that the children of God are actuated by his Spirit to do whatever is to be done. Also, that they are drawn by him, so as out of unwilling to be made willing.[21]

Calvin regarded the drawing of God to be something more than an offer of assistance for the weak or some other enticement to act. Calvin saw this drawing as a divine work actuating human will, a work without which the will would not respond positively to a divine offer.

Calvin also explains the drawing of God in his *Commentary on the Gospel According to John:* "... Christ declares that the doctrine of the Gospel, though it is preached to all without exception, cannot be embraced by all, but that a new understanding and a new perception are requisite; and, therefore, that faith does not depend on the will of men, but that it is God who gives it."[22]

This comment is part of Calvin's exposition of Jesus' statement that "no man can come to me, unless the Father, who hath sent me, draw him" (John 6:44). With respect to the clause "unless the Father . . . draw him," Calvin writes:

> To "come to Christ" being here used metaphorically for "believing," the Evangelist, in order to carry out the metaphor in the apposite clause, says that those persons are "drawn" whose understandings God enlightens, and whose hearts he bends and forms to the obedience of Christ. . . . we ought not to wonder if many refuse to embrace the Gospel; because no man will ever of himself be able to come to Christ, but God must first approach him by his Spirit; and hence it follows that all are not "drawn," but that God bestows this grace on those whom he has elected. True, indeed, as to the kind of "drawing," it is not violent, so as to compel men by external force; but still it is a powerful impulse of the

Related Works about Calvin

de Greef, Wulfert. *The Writings of John Calvin: An Introductory Guide.* Translated by Lyle D. Bierma. Grand Rapids: Baker / Leicester: Apollos, 1993.

James, Frank, III, ed. *John Calvin.* In *Christian History* 5, 4 (1986).

McGrath, Alister E. *A Life of John Calvin.* Oxford: Blackwell, 1990 / Grand Rapids: Baker, 1995.

Sproul, R. C., Jr., ed. "John Calvin." *Tabletalk* 19 (October 1995).

Wendel, François. *Calvin: Origins and Development of His Religious Thought.* Translated by Philip Mairet. 1963. Reprint. Grand Rapids: Baker, 1997.

Holy Spirit, which makes men willing who formerly were unwilling and reluctant. It is a false and profane assertion, therefore, that none are *drawn* but those who are willing to be "drawn," as if man made himself obedient to God by his own efforts; for the willingness with which men follow God is what they already have from himself, who has formed their hearts to obey him.[23]

Later Calvin comments on a similar statement by Jesus, that no one can come to him unless it is *given* to the person by the Father (John 6:65): "He now uses the word *give* instead of the word . . . he formerly used, *draw;* by which he means that there is no other reason why God *draws,* than because out of free grace he loves us; for what we obtain by the gift and grace of God, no man procures for himself by his own industry."[24]

The Teaching of Paul

In his commentary on the Epistle to the Ephesians, Calvin links the drawing of God with the quickening of the Holy Spirit. The quickening of the Spirit is his work on those who were "dead in trespasses and sins" (Eph. 2:1). Calvin defines this condition of spiritual death as "nothing else than the alienation of the soul from God."[25] He says we are all born dead and remain in that state of spiritual death until we are made partakers of the life of Christ.

He accuses Rome of teaching that outside of Christ we are but half-dead. Since Paul describes this condition of spiritual death as walking according to the course of this world, Calvin argues that we formerly lived according to the desire of the fallen nature. "'The flesh' means here [Eph. 2:3] the disposition, or what is called the inclination of the nature," writes Calvin. "This is a remarkable passage against the Pelagians and all who deny original sin. What dwells naturally in all is certainly original; but Paul teaches that we are all naturally liable to condemnation. Therefore sin dwells in us, for God does not condemn the innocent. The Pelagians quibbled that sin spread from Adam to the whole human race, not by derivation, but by imitation. But Paul affirms that we are born with sin, as serpents bring their venom from the womb."[26]

From this, Calvin moves to an exposition of Ephesians 2:4–7, declaring that the substance of the text is that the Ephesians were delivered from destruction by God. Calvin says the passage teaches that "there is no other life of the soul than that which is breathed into us by Christ."[27]

Then Calvin expounds verses 8–10: "For by grace have ye been saved through faith; and that not of yourselves: it is the gift of God: not of works, lest any man should boast. For we are his work, created in Christ Jesus for good works, which God afore prepared that we should walk in them."[28]

This passage stresses God's grace. Paul says that it is not "of yourselves," but the result of the work of God. Calvin declares: ". . . all the good works which we possess are the fruit of regeneration. Hence it follows that works themselves are a part of grace. When he says that we are the work of God, it is not to be taken of general creation, by which we men are born, but he asserts that we are new creatures who are formed to righteousness by the Spirit of Christ and not by our own power. . . . Everything in us that is good, therefore, is the supernatural work of God."[29]

From this brief exposition Calvin draws conclusions that relate directly to the question of free will:

> What remains now for free-will, if all the good works which proceed from us have been received from the Spirit of God? Let godly readers weigh carefully the apostle's words. He does not say that we are assisted by God. He does not say that the will is prepared, and has then to proceed in its own strength. He does not say that the power of choosing aright is bestowed upon us, and that we have afterwards to make our own choice. . . . But he says that we are God's work, and that everything good in us is His creation. . . . It is not the mere power of choosing aright, or some indefinable preparation, or assistance, but the right will itself, which is His workmanship. . . . Whoever, then, makes the very smallest claim for man, apart from the grace of God, allows him to that extent ability to procure salvation.[30]

Finally we turn to Calvin's commentary on the Epistle to the Romans and his exposition of chapter 9. When Paul speaks of the election of Jacob over Esau before either of their births, he says, "... it is not of him that willeth. ..." (Rom. 9:16 KJV). Calvin elaborates on this passage:

> Paul deduces from this statement the incontrovertible conclusion that our election is to be attributed neither to our diligence, zeal, nor efforts, but is to be ascribed entirely to the counsel of God. Let no one think that those who are elected are chosen because they are deserving, or because they have in any way won for themselves the favour of God, or even because they possessed a grain of worthiness by which God might be moved to act. The simple view which we are to take is that our being counted among the elect is independent either of our will or [of] our efforts. ... It is rather to be attributed wholly to the divine goodness, which freely takes those who neither will to achieve, nor strive for, nor even think of such a thing.[31]

Calvin then responds to the Pelagian interpretation of Romans 9 by again appealing to Augustine:

> Pelagius has attempted to evade this assertion of Paul by another quibbling and quite worthless objection. He has maintained that our election does not depend on willing and running alone, since the mercy of God assists us. Augustine, however, has refuted him both effectively and astutely. If it is denied that the will of man is the cause of election, because it is a partial and not the sole cause, so we may also say on the other hand that election is not dependent on God's mercy, but on willing and running. Where there is mutual co-operation there will also be reciprocal praise. But this latter proposition falls incontrovertibly by its own absurdity.[32]

Francis Turretin

In the seventeenth century Calvinism was challenged by other schools of thought that we will consider later. This period is often called the age of Protestant scholasticism. It was also a period when creeds were formulated. *The Westminster Confession,* for example, follows closely Calvin's view of the will. Perhaps the most articulate of Calvin's successors in Geneva was Francis Turretin. He takes up the question of free will in his *Institutes of Elenctic Theology.*

Turretin asks if, in the first moment of conversion, man is merely passive or if he cooperates in some measure with the grace of God. He affirms the former (monergism) and denies the latter (synergism). Turretin says: "This question lies between us and the Romanists, Socinians, Remonstrants and other offshoots of the Pelagians and Semipelagians who, not to injure or remove the free will of man in calling, maintain that it has a certain cooperation (*synergeian*) and concourse with the grace of God. Hence they are called Synergists."[33]

Turretin affirmed with Calvin, Luther, and Augustine that *after* the initial step of regeneration, in the second stage of conversion, man is certainly active. It is the man who does the believing. The issue for Turretin, however, is the *first* stage of conversion. Rome agrees that without prevenient grace man could not be converted. The issue is whether or not man in his fallen condition, prior to the grace of regeneration, can cooperate with prevenient grace. Turretin does not deny that the sinner can do certain things to *prepare* himself for the grace of regeneration, such as going to church and listening to the preaching of the word. Turretin says:

> . . . the question is whether in the very moment of conversion and as to the steps of the thing, man has anything from himself with which he can cooperate with efficacious grace so that the work can be ascribed not only to grace, but also to free will excited by grace. . . . The [orthodox] recognize no efficient cause properly so called other than God himself regenerating or the Spirit of regeneration. And they make man to be regenerated the merely passive subject of the regenerating Spirit and of the new qualities infused by him (although after the new qualities have already been infused, he holds himself as the free active instrument of his own actions).[34]

Then Turretin reviews canon 4 of the sixth session of the Council of Trent, which reads: "If anyone says that the free will of man moved and excited by God cooperates not at all, by assenting to God exciting and calling, by which it disposes and prepares itself for obtaining the grace of justification and cannot dissent if it wishes, but as an inanimate something does not act at all and is merely passive, let him be anathema."[35]

Turretin catches the ambiguity, if not confusion, in this canon and asks the critical question: What is meant by God's "exciting" man? Turretin responds:

> . . . because our adversaries frequently distinguish grace into "exciting and assisting, operating and cooperating, prevenient and subsequent," we must before all things ascertain in what sense it can either be admitted or ought to be rejected. If by exciting, operating and prevenient grace, they understand the first movement of efficacious grace by which we are excited from the death of sin to a new life and really converted before any cooperation and concourse of our will; and by assisting, cooperating, and subsequent, its second movement, which is cooperated with by the converted and assists them to act, we would readily admit this distinction.[36]

Turretin acknowledges that he would agree with this definition of exciting grace and asserts that it would be altogether consistent with the thought of Augustine as well. But he concludes that this is not what Rome means. The phrase "is employed in a different sense by them, so that by exciting, prevenient and operating, they mean only sufficient grace acting by illumination and moral suasion (which does not subject the free will to itself so as to efficaciously incline and determine it to acting, but is subjected to the free will so that it is always in its power to receive or reject that grace; to consent to or dissent from it), and by cooperating grace, that which cooperates with the yet unconverted will, and with which in turn the will not as yet converted cooperates."[37]

After citing Roman Catholic scholars like Robert Bellarmine who confirm his understanding of Trent, Turretin turns his attention to another pivotal issue. He seeks to answer this question: "Whether efficacious grace operates only by a certain moral suasion which man is able either to receive or to reject. Or whether it operates by an invincible and omnipotent suasion which the will of man cannot resist."[38] In other words, is regenerating grace effectual or resistible? Turretin calls this "the principal hinge of the controversy, agitated after the Romanists by the Arminians concerning the mode of conversion."[39] Here he has in mind the controversy that culminated in the Synod of Dort. He says:

> . . . the Arminians seem to grant all things to grace and confess that free will can do nothing of itself. But when they come to an explanation of the mode, according to which grace acts, then they maintain that it always so operates that man is free either to admit it or to reject it, either to draw or not to draw the bolt. Hence of two to whom the same grace is offered, if one is converted while the other remains unbelieving, the reason is not to be found (according to them) in the grace (which is the same), but in the disposition of the subject or man, because the one draws the bolt, the other does not (i.e., one rejects the grace which the other admits). Thus what they seem to give largely with one hand (preaching that the beginning, progress and complement of all our good is from grace), they secretly steal away with the other, maintaining that the mode of that operation is "resistible" (under which word they hide the consent and cooperation of the will by which man can always either reject or receive grace—i.e., make himself to differ.)[40]

Turretin grants that men can and do resist God's grace. What *irresistible* means is that the grace of regeneration accomplishes what God intends. It is efficacious. Man, under its influence, is unable to conquer or overcome the power of grace. This grace is irresistible in that it is a divine act of re-creation in which God gives the sinner a new heart. God imparts to the sinner the very act of willing.

Turretin concludes: ". . . if God not only appeals to and exhorts, but himself works (*energei*) in us; not only works the power but the very act of willing and believing, who does not see that his action is irresistible which necessarily produces its own effect? For if man can always resist or can actually resist, this would undoubtedly be done because the will willed to resist. And yet how can the will will to resist (i.e., be unwilling to admit grace, in which God efficaciously works to will)?"[41]

For Turretin, as for Calvin and Luther, the "irresistibility" of grace is what makes it so gracious. Irresistible grace denies the converted sinner any basis for boasting. This grace insures the *sola* of *sola gratia* and *sola fide*. This grace underlies the affirmation that, in the final analysis, salvation is of the Lord.

*All unregenerate persons
have freedom of will,
and a capability
of resisting the Holy Spirit,
of rejecting the proffered
grace of God, . . .
and of not opening to Him who
knocks at the door of the heart;
and these things
they can actually do.*

James Arminius

6

We Are Free to Believe:
James Arminius

J ames Arminius was emphatic in his rejection of Pelagianism, particularly with respect to the fall of Adam. The fall leaves man in a ruined state, under the dominion of sin. Arminius declares: "In this state, the Free Will of man towards the True Good is not only wounded, maimed, infirm, bent, and weakened *[attenuatem]*; but it is also imprisoned *[captivatum]*, destroyed, and lost. And its powers are not only debilitated and useless unless they be assisted by grace, but it has no powers whatever except such as are excited by Divine grace. . . ."[1]

In the perennial debate between so-called Calvinism and Arminianism, the estranged parties have frequently misrepresented each other. They construct straw men, then brandish the swords of polemics against caricatures, not unlike collective Don Quixotes tilting at windmills. As a Calvinist I frequently hear criticisms of Calvinistic thought that I would heartily agree with if indeed they represented Calvinism. So, I am sure, the disciples of Arminius suffer the same fate and become equally frustrated. Arminius himself came from a Calvinistic framework and embraced many tenets of historic Calvinism. He frequently complained, in a mild spirit, of the manifold ways in which he was misrepresented. He loved the works of Augustine and in many respects earnestly sought to champion the Augustinian cause.

The above citation from one of Arminius's works demonstrates how seriously he regards the depths of the fall. He is not satisfied to declare that man's will was merely wounded or weakened. He insists that it was "imprisoned, destroyed, and lost." The language of Augustine, Martin Luther, or John Calvin is scarcely stronger than that of Arminius.

Indeed, to show his agreement with Augustine, Arminius goes on to say: "For Christ has said, 'Without me ye can do nothing' [John 15:5]. St. Augustine, after having diligently meditated upon each word in this passage, speaks thus: 'Christ does not say, "Without me ye can do *but little";* neither does He say, "Without me ye cannot do *any arduous thing,"* nor "Without me ye can do it with difficulty": But He says, "Without me ye can do *nothing!"* Nor does He say, "Without me ye cannot *complete [perficere]* any thing"; but "Without me ye can do *nothing.""*[2]

So far Arminius clearly seems to agree with Augustine, Luther, and Calvin. He affirms the ruination of the will, which is left in a state of captivity and can avail nothing apart from the grace of God. It would seem, then, that the debate between historic Calvinism and Arminianism is but a tempest in a teapot, resulting from a serious misunderstanding between the parties. The point at issue will appear later, however, as we consider the nature of grace and how it liberates man from his bondage to sin.

Effects of the Fall

Arminius distinguishes among three aspects of fallen man: his mind, his affections, and his life. Of the mind Arminius says:

The Mind of man, in this state, is dark, destitute of the saving knowledge of God, and, according to the Apostle, incapable of those things which belong to the Spirit of God: For "the animal man has no perception of the things of the Spirit of God" (1 Cor. 2:14); in which passage man is called "animal," not from the animal body, but from *anima,* the soul itself, which is the most noble part of man, but which is so encompassed about with the

Events in the Life of Arminius
1560 Born in Oudewater, The Netherlands
1582 Began theological studies in Geneva
1587 Began ministry in Amsterdam
1588 Ordained
1590 Married Lijsbet Reael
1603 Joined theological faculty in Leiden
1609 Died in Leiden

clouds of ignorance, as to be distinguished by the epithets of "vain" and "foolish"; and men themselves, thus darkened in their minds, are denominated "mad" *[amentes]* or foolish, "fools," and even "darkness" itself (Rom. 1:21–22; Eph. 4:17–18; Titus 3:3; Eph. 5:8).[3]

This dark state of the mind is exacerbated by the heart or affections, which further plunge human thinking into corruption: "To this Darkness of the Mind succeeds the Perverseness of the Affections and of the Heart, according to which it hates and has an aversion to that which is truly good and pleasing to God; but it loves and pursues what is evil."[4]

Arminius cites numerous biblical quotations in support of his view of the effects of sin. Together, the darkness of the mind and the perversity of the heart leave men morally impotent:

> Exactly correspondent to this Darkness of the Mind, and Perverseness of the Heart, is the utter Weakness *[impotentia]* of all the Powers to perform that which is truly good, and to omit the perpetration of that which is evil, in a due mode and from a due end and cause. . . .
>
> To these let the consideration of the whole of the Life of Man who is placed *[constituti]* under sin, be added, of which the Scriptures exhibit to us the most luminous descriptions; and it will be evident, that nothing can be spoken more truly concerning man in this state, than that he is altogether dead in sin (Rom. 3:10–19).[5]

Arminius not only affirms the bondage of the will, but insists that natural man, being dead in sin, exists in a state of moral inability or impotence. What more could an Augustinian or Calvinist hope for from a theologian? Arminius then declares that the only remedy for man's fallen condition is the gracious operation of God's Spirit. The will of man is not free to do any good unless it is made free or liberated by the Son of God through the Spirit of God. Arminius describes the Spirit's operation in the following terms:

> . . . a new light and knowledge of God and Christ, and of the Divine Will, have been kindled in his mind; and . . . new affections, inclinations and motions agreeing with the law of God, have been excited in his heart, and new powers have been produced [ingeneratae] in him. . . . [Then,] being liberated from the kingdom of darkness, and being now made "light in the Lord" (Eph. 5:8) he understands the true and saving Good; that, after the hardness of his stony heart has been changed into the softness of flesh, . . . he loves and embraces that which is good, just, and holy; and that, being made capable [potens] in Christ, co-operating now with God he prosecutes the Good which he knows and loves, and he begins himself to perform it in deed. But this, whatever it may be of knowledge, holiness and power, is all begotten within him by the Holy Spirit. . . .[6]

Again it seems that Arminius is merely echoing the teaching of Luther and Calvin. He affirms the absolute necessity of grace for man to turn to the good, and he even speaks of the Holy Spirit working "within" man to accomplish all of this.

Then Arminius makes an observation that sounds like a sudden departure from Reformation thought. He declares that "this work of regeneration and illumination is not completed in one moment; but . . . it is advanced and promoted, from time to time, by daily increase."[7] When Arminius expands on this point, he seems to mean that what is begun in regeneration is continued in the process of life-long sanctification. For example, the divine illumination that occurs at the onset of conversion is a work that continues through the Christian pilgrimage.

What is jarring here is Arminius's reference to regeneration's not being completed in one moment. Perhaps this is a mere slip of the pen, intended to convey the idea that the *fruit* of regeneration is ongoing. If he means that the work of regeneration itself is not instantaneous but gradual, then he sets himself in opposition to Reformation thought.

The beginning of the work of grace is called *preventing grace* or more popularly *prevenient grace,* referring to the grace that comes before conversion and on which conversion depends. Arminius first quotes Augustine, then Bernardus:

> "Subsequent or *following* Grace does indeed assist the good purpose of man; but this good purpose would have no existence unless through preceding or *preventing* Grace. And though the desire of man, which is called *good,* be assisted by Grace when it begins to be; yet it does not begin without Grace, but is inspired by Him. . . ."
>
> "'What then,' you ask, 'does Free Will do?' I reply with brevity, 'It saves.' Take away *Free Will,* and nothing will be left to be saved: Take away *Grace,* and nothing will be left as the source of salvation. This work [of salvation] cannot be effected without two parties: One, from whom it may come; The Other, to whom or in whom it may be [wrought.] God is the Author of salvation: Free Will is only capable *[tantum capere]* of being saved. No one, except God, is able to bestow salvation; and nothing, except Free Will, is capable of receiving it."[8]

The term *preventing grace* is open to misunderstanding. *To prevent* in modern usage usually means "to keep something from happening." This is not how Arminius uses the term. The word *prevent* derives from the Latin *venio,* which means simply "to come." The prefix *pre* means "before." Therefore, *preventing grace* does not keep salvation from happening but necessarily "comes before" salvation.

Later Arminius addresses the distinction commonly found in Reformed theology between the *external* and *internal* calls of God. The external or outward call usually refers to the preaching of the gospel that men hear with their ears. The internal call refers to the operation of the Spirit of God within man, whereby he calls them internally. It is not a mere outward wooing, enticing, pleading, or drawing.

The Point of Departure

Arminius declares that "internal vocation is granted *[contingit]* even to those who do not comply with the call."[9] Here, at last, we see the critical point of departure from the view of Luther and Calvin. For the Reformers, the internal call is effectual. That is, all whom God calls internally comply with his call. This sets the stage for the debate over the resistible or irresistible grace of regeneration. Arminius declares: "All unregenerate persons have freedom of will, and a capability of resisting the Holy Spirit, of rejecting the proffered grace of God, of despising the counsel of God against themselves, of refusing to accept the Gospel of grace, and of not opening to Him who knocks at the door of the heart; and these things they can actually do, without any difference of *the Elect* and of *the Reprobate*."[10]

Arminius makes it clear that prevenient grace is resistible. This grace is necessary for salvation, but does not insure that salvation will ensue. Grace is a *necessary condition* for salvation, but not a *sufficient condition* for salvation. Arminius distinguishes between sufficient and efficient grace: "Sufficient grace must necessarily be laid down; yet this sufficient grace, through the fault of him to whom it is granted *[contingit]*, does not [always] obtain its effect. Were the fact otherwise, the justice of God could not be defended in his condemning those who do not believe."[11]

Prevenient grace is "sufficient" in that it provides everything the sinner needs in order to be saved. The sinner is unable to do the good without it. We can see here that Arminius's chief concern is to defend the justice of God.

If only irresistible grace is given, then in the final analysis God determines who will and who will not be saved. The unspoken question is this: If the sinner cannot respond to the gospel without irresistible grace and if this grace is not given to all, then how can God justly condemn those to whom he has not given it?

Arminius goes on to say: "The efficacy of saving grace is not consistent with that omnipotent act of God, by which He so inwardly acts in the heart and mind of man, that he on whom that act is impressed cannot do any other than consent to God who calls him. Or, which is the same thing, grace is not an irresistible force."[12]

> **Related Works by Arminius**
>
> *Certain Articles to Be Diligently Examined and Weighed.* In *The Works of James Arminius: The London Edition.* 3 vols. Grand Rapids: Baker, 1986. 2:706–54.
> *The Public Disputations of James Arminius.* In *The Works of James Arminius: The London Edition.* 3 vols. Grand Rapids: Baker, 1986. 2:72–264.

A bit earlier Arminius said that prevenient grace is sufficient but not efficient. It does not always obtain its effect. At this point he laid the *fault* with men rather than with God. The failure to acquiesce in this sufficient grace is a fault. Arminius does not say that the assent to prevenient grace is a virtue, but he strongly implies it. If failure to assent is a fault, then to assent is a virtue. If it is not virtue, it is at the very least decisive to the outcome. In the final analysis the good outcome is contingent or dependent on what the person does or does not do.

Is Arminius's view of regeneration monergistic or synergistic? To answer this question we must first understand what is meant by *regeneration.* Is regeneration the same as prevenient grace? If prevenient grace always enables the sinner to assent to grace, then Arminius's view is monergistic in this regard. For Arminius prevenient grace seems to be irresistible to the degree that it effectively liberates the sinner from his moral bondage or impotency. Prior to receiving prevenient grace, man is dead and utterly unable to choose the good. After receiving this grace, the sinner is able to do what he was previously unable to do. In this sense, prevenient grace is monergistic and irresistible.

But what Arminius calls the inward vocation or call of God is neither monergistic nor irresistible. He says: "Those who are obedient to the vocation or call of God, freely yield their assent to grace; yet they are previously excited, impelled, drawn and assisted by grace. And in the very moment in which they actually assent, they possess the capability of not assenting."[13]

Prevenient grace, then, makes man *able* to assent to Christ but not necessarily *willing*. The sinner is now able to will, but he is not yet willing to do so. The ability to will is the result of a monergistic, irresistible work of the Holy Spirit, but the actual willing is the synergistic work of the sinner cooperating with God's prevenient grace. Giving grace is the work of God alone; assenting to it is the work of man, who now has the power to cooperate or not cooperate with it.

Arminius's view differs sharply from the Augustinian and Reformed view, which insists that the monergistic work of regeneration makes the sinner not only able to will but also willing. To be sure, it is still the sinner who wills, but he wills because God has changed the disposition of his heart. Arminius says: "In the very commencement of his conversion, man conducts himself in a purely passive manner; that is, though, by a vital act, that is, by feeling *[sensu]*, he has a perception of the grace which calls him, yet he can do no other than receive it and feel it. But, when he feels grace affecting or inclining his mind and heart, he freely assents to it, so that he is able at the same time to with-hold his assent."[14]

Arminius makes it clear that, at the commencement of the work of salvation, man is passive. The exciting of grace on the soul is monergistic. The response to this exciting is synergistic, in that one can freely assent to it or withhold assent. Francis Turretin notes this distinction in Arminius:

> The question is not whether grace is resistible in respect of the intellect or affections; for the Arminians confess that the intellect of man is irresistibly enlightened and his affections irresistibly excited and affected with the sense of grace. But it is treated of the will alone, which they maintain is always moved resistibly, so that its assent remains always free. There is granted indeed irresistibly the power to believe and convert itself, but the very act of believing and converting itself can be put forth or hindered by the human will because they hold that there is in it an essential indifference *(adiaphorian)* as to admitting or rejecting grace. . . . Thus we strenuously deny that efficacious grace is resistible in this sense. . . .

> ... Nay, we maintain that efficacious grace so works in man that although he cannot help resisting from the beginning, still he can never resist it so far as to finally overcome it and hinder the work of conversion.[15]

The Rich Man and the Beggar

In answering a list of theological articles written against his views, Arminius complains at several points that he has been misunderstood or misrepresented. He was accused of teaching that faith is not the pure gift of God but depends partly on grace and partly on free will. He answered that he never said faith was not the pure gift of God, and he offered in response what he calls a *simile:*

> A rich man bestows, on a poor and famishing beggar, alms by which he may be able to maintain himself and his family. Does it cease to be a pure gift, because the beggar extends his hand to receive it? Can it be said with propriety, that "the alms depended partly on *the liberality* of the Donor, and partly on *the liberty* of the Receiver," though the latter would not have possessed the alms unless he had received it by stretching out his hand? Can it be correctly said, *because the beggar is always prepared to receive,* that "he can have the alms, or not have it, just as he pleases?" If these assertions cannot be truly made about a beggar who receives alms, how much less can they be made about the gift of faith, for the receiving of which far more acts of Divine Grace are required![16]

In Arminius's simile it is hard to imagine a destitute beggar not assenting to such a gracious gift. But the fact remains that, to receive the alms, the beggar, while still destitute, must stretch out his hand. At the same time, he stretches out his hand because he wants to do so.

To receive the gift of faith, according to Calvinism, the sinner also must stretch out his hand. But he does so only because God has so changed the disposition of his heart that he will most certainly stretch out his hand. By the irresistible work of grace, he will do nothing else except stretch out his hand. Not that he cannot not stretch out his hand even if he does not want to, but that he cannot not want to stretch out his hand.

In Arminius's simile, the beggar could conceivably be so obstreperous as to refuse the alms offered. In Augustinianism, this very obstinacy is effectively conquered by irresistible grace. For Calvin, the grace of God extends not only to the alms, but also to the very stretching out of the hand. For Arminius, the beggar possesses the natural power to stretch out his hand.

One irony of history is that Arminius took this position in the midst of an effort initially designed to defend Calvinism. He held Calvin and his work in high regard. At one point Arminius said:

> Next to the study of the Scriptures which I earnestly inculcate, I exhort my pupils to peruse Calvin's *Commentaries,* which I extol in loftier terms than Helmich himself [a Dutch divine, 1551–1608]; for I affirm that he excels beyond comparison *(incomparabilem esse)* in the interpretation of Scripture, and that his commentaries ought to be more highly valued than all that is handed down to us by the library of the fathers; so that I acknowledge him to have possessed above most others, or rather above all other men, what may be called an eminent spirit of prophecy *(spiritum aliquem prophetiae eximium).* His *Institutes* ought to be studied after the [Heidelberg] Catechism, as containing a fuller explanation, but with discrimination *(cum delectu),* like the writings of all men.[17]

Arminius had been educated at the University of Leiden in the Netherlands from 1576 to 1582. After graduation he was sent to Geneva for further study. He took a pastorate in Amsterdam in 1588. In 1603 he was appointed professor of theology at Leiden.

In 1589 Arminius was asked to defend the doctrine of supralapsarianism against two ministers of Delft. As he prepared, he began to doubt not only supralapsarianism, but the whole doctrine of unconditional predestination. In this crucible his views on human freedom were forged. Soon a fierce controversy erupted between Arminius and his supralapsarian colleague, Franciscus

Gomarus, escalating into a national debate with political ramifications throughout Holland. After Arminius died in 1609, his views were systematized by his pupil and successor at Leiden, Simon Episcopius.[18]

The Remonstrants

In 1610 followers of Arminius and Episcopius, led by the statesman Johan van Oldenbarneveldt, drew up a statement of faith called *The Remonstrance*, which gave their party the name *Remonstrants*.[19] The Remonstrants presented their views in a series of five articles that often appear under the title *Articuli Arminiani sive remonstrantia.* Roger Nicole summarizes these five articles as follows:

> **Related Works about Arminius**
>
> Bangs, Carl. *Arminius: A Study in the Dutch Reformation.* 1971. 2d ed. Grand Rapids: Asbury / Zondervan, 1985.
>
> Bangs, Carl. "Introduction." In James Arminius, *The Works of James Arminius: The London Edition.* 3 vols. Grand Rapids: Baker, 1986. 1:vii–xxix.
>
> Muller, Richard A. *God, Creation, and Providence in the Thought of Jacob Arminius: Sources and Directions of Scholastic Protestantism in the Era of Early Orthodoxy.* Grand Rapids: Baker, 1991.

1. God elects or reproves on the basis of foreseen faith or unbelief.
2. Christ died for all men and for every man, although only believers are saved.
3. Man is so depraved that divine grace is necessary unto faith or any good deed.
4. This grace may be resisted.
5. Whether all who are truly regenerate will certainly persevere in the faith is a point which needs further investigation.[20]

The two articles that bear most heavily on the issues under consideration in this volume are articles 3 and 4:

> 3. . . . man does not have saving faith of himself nor by the power of his own free will, since he in the state of apostasy and sin cannot of and through himself think, will or do any good which is truly good (such as is especially saving faith); but . . . it

is necessary that he be regenerated by God, in Christ, through his Holy Spirit, and renewed in understanding, affections or will, and all powers, in order that he may rightly understand, meditate upon, will, and perform that which is truly good, according to the word of Christ, "Without me ye can do nothing" (John 15:5).

4. . . . this grace of God is the commencement, progression, and completion of all good, also in so far that regenerate man cannot, apart from this prevenient or assisting, awakening, consequent and cooperating grace, think, will or do the good or resist any temptations to evil; so that all good works or activities which can be conceived must be ascribed to the grace of God in Christ. But with respect to the mode of this grace, it is not irresistible, since it is written concerning many that they resisted the Holy Spirit (Acts 7[:51] and elsewhere in many places).[21]

In 1611 a conference was held in Holland allowing the Remonstrants to interact with representatives of their opposition. The opposition presented *The Counter Remonstrance,* consisting of seven articles in response to the controverted points. *The Counter Remonstrance* contained the following statements:

3. . . . God in his election has not looked to the faith or conversion of his elect, nor to the right use of his gifts, as the grounds of election; but . . . on the contrary He in his eternal and immutable counsel has purposed and decreed to bestow faith and perseverance in godliness and thus to save those whom He according to his good pleasure has chosen to salvation. . . .

5. . . . furthermore to the same end God the Lord has his holy gospel preached, and . . . the Holy Spirit externally through the preaching of that same gospel and internally through a special grace works so powerfully in the hearts of God's elect, that He illumines their minds, transforms and renews their wills, removing the heart of stone and giving them a heart of flesh, in such a manner that by these means they not only receive power to convert themselves and believe but also actually and willingly do repent and believe.[22]

The Synod of Dort

The debate continued, and a major synod was convened in the city of Dordrecht (or Dort) in November 1618. In addition to Dutch participants, delegates were also included from England, Germany, and Switzerland. The Synod of Dort, which concluded in May 1619, condemned Arminianism and adopted distinctive canons reaffirming historic Calvinism. *The Canons of Dort* were then received along with the *Heidelberg Catechism* and the *Belgic Confession.*

At the synod the Remonstrants reaffirmed their belief that man in his fallen state lacks the power or freedom to will any saving good, but that the grace by which men are converted is resistible. God's grace is *sufficient* for faith and conversion, but not irresistibly *efficient.* They declared:

> The efficacious grace by which anyone is converted is not irresistible; and though God so influences the will by the Word and the internal operation of His Spirit that He both confers the strength to believe or supernatural powers, and actually causes man to believe—yet man is able of himself to despise that grace and not to believe, and therefore to perish through his own fault.
>
> Although according to the most free will of God the disparity of divine grace is very great, nevertheless the Holy Spirit confers, or is ready to confer, as much grace to all men and to each man to whom the Word of God is preached as is sufficient for promoting the conversion of men in its steps. Therefore sufficient grace for faith and conversion falls to the lot not only of those whom God is said to will to save according to the decree of absolute election, but also of those who are not actually converted.[23]

In April 1619 the synod adopted canons that set forth the faith of the Reformed churches, along with a list of errors that they rejected. *The Canons of Dort* categorically rejected the prescient view of election so common among semi-Pelagians, and affirmed what is often called "unconditional election." With respect to the operation of free will and the efficacy of grace, the synod had much to say with respect to Arminianism. What follows is a brief section of the canons regarding this point of contention:

> ... that others who are called by the gospel obey the call and are converted is not to be ascribed to the proper exercise of free will, whereby one distinguishes himself above others equally furnished with grace sufficient for faith and conversion (as the proud heresy of Pelagius maintains); but it must be wholly ascribed to God, who, as He has chosen His own from eternity in Christ, so He calls them effectually in time, confers upon them faith and repentance, rescues them from the power of darkness, and translates them into the kingdom of His own Son; that they may show forth the praises of Him who has called them out of darkness into His marvelous light, and may glory not in themselves but in the Lord, according to the testimony of the apostles in various places.[24]

This article accents the monergistic work of God, to whom conversion is "wholly ascribed." It is noteworthy that *The Canons* relate the rejection of this monergism to the heresy of Pelagius. *The Canons* go on to assert:

> But when God accomplishes His good pleasure in the elect, or works in them true conversion, He not only causes the gospel to be externally preached to them, and powerfully illuminates their minds by His Holy Spirit, that they may rightly understand and discern the things of the Spirit of God; but by the efficacy of the same regenerating Spirit He pervades the inmost recesses of man; He opens the closed and softens the hardened heart, and circumcises that which was uncircumcised; infuses new qualities into the will, which, though heretofore dead, He quickens; from being evil, disobedient, and refractory, He renders it good, obedient, and pliable; actuates and strengthens it, that like a good tree, it may bring forth the fruits of good actions.
>
> And this is that regeneration ... which God works in us without our aid. But this is in no wise effected merely by the external preaching of the gospel, by moral suasion, or [by] such a mode of operation that, after God has performed His part, it still remains in the power of man to be regenerated or not, to be converted or to continue unconverted; but it is evidently a supernatural work, most powerful, and at the same time most delightful, astonish-

ing, mysterious, and ineffable; not inferior in efficacy to creation or the resurrection from the dead, . . . so that all in whose heart God works in this marvelous manner are certainly, infallibly, and effectually regenerated, and do actually believe. Whereupon the will thus renewed is not only actuated and influenced by God, but in consequence of this influence becomes itself active. Wherefore also man himself is rightly said to believe and repent by virtue of that grace received.[25]

These canons make abundantly clear the difference between the views of Arminius and the Remonstrants and the views of classical Reformed theology. The issue of the efficacy of grace is in the final analysis crucial to the Reformation principle of *sola gratia.*

In addition to the canons that affirm the doctrines of Dort, the synod listed corresponding errors to be rejected.

The true doctrine having been explained, the Synod rejects the errors of those: . . .

Who teach: That in the true conversion of man no new qualities, powers, or gifts can be infused by God into the will, and that therefore faith, through which we are first converted and because of which we are called believers, is not a quality or gift infused by God but only an act of man, and that it cannot be said to be a gift, except in respect of the power to attain to this faith. . . .

Who teach: That the grace whereby we are converted to God is only a gentle advising, or (as others explain it) that this is the noblest manner of working in the conversion of man, and that this manner of working, which consists in advising, is most in harmony with man's nature; and that there is no reason why this advising grace alone should not be sufficient to make the natural man spiritual; indeed, that God does not produce the consent of the will except through this manner of advising; and that the power of the divine working, whereby it surpasses the working of Satan, consists in this that God promises eternal, while Satan promises only temporal goods. But this is altogether Pelagian and contrary to the whole Scripture. . . .

Who teach: That God in the regeneration of man does not use such powers of His omnipotence as potently and infallibly bend man's will to faith and conversion; but that all the works of grace having been accomplished, which God employs to convert man, man may yet so resist God and the Holy Spirit, when God intends man's regeneration and wills to regenerate him, and indeed that man often does so resist that he prevents entirely his regeneration, and that it therefore remains in man's power to be regenerated or not. For this is nothing less than the denial of all the efficiency of God's grace in our conversion, and the subjecting of the working of Almighty God to the will of man, which is contrary to the apostles. . . . [26]

Repeatedly the Synod of Dort charges the Remonstrants with teaching the doctrines of Pelagianism. Is not this charge overly severe and unfair? Both Arminius and the Remonstrants sought to distance themselves from pure Pelagianism. Arminianism is often said to be semi-Pelagian, but not, strictly speaking, Pelagian. What the fathers of Dort probably had in mind is the link between semi-Pelagianism and Pelagianism that renders the semi-Pelagian unable to escape the fundamental thesis of Pelagianism.

Modern Arminianism

The Synod of Dort did not destroy the Arminian movement. It spread throughout the Continent and later into Colonial America. It survives to this day and currently enjoys a strong resurgence. In 1989 Clark H. Pinnock edited *The Grace of God, the Will of Man*, a volume designed to make the case for Arminianism.

In his own essay, in which he chronicles his personal pilgrimage from Calvinism to Arminianism, Pinnock observes: "A theological shift is underway among evangelicals as well as other Christians away from determinism as regards the rule and salvation of God and in the direction of an orientation more favorable to a dynamic personal relationship between God, the world, and God's human creatures. The trend began, I believe, because of a fresh and faithful reading of the Bible in dialogue with modern culture, which places emphasis on autonomy, temporality, and historical change."[27]

Pinnock welcomes this trend and contends that great theologians often change their minds. He cites Karl Barth as an example, referring to Barth as "undoubtedly the greatest theologian of our century."[28] In assessing this current drift or trend in evangelical theology, he further notes: "At the same time, however, the Calvinists continue to be major players in the evangelical coalition, even though their dominance has lessened. They pretty well control the teaching of theology in the large evangelical seminaries; they own and operate the largest book-publishing houses; and in large part they manage the inerrancy movement. This means they are strong where it counts—in the area of intellectual leadership and property. . . . Although there are many Arminian thinkers in apologetics, missiology, and the practice of ministry, there are only a few evangelical theologians ready to go to bat for non-Augustinian opinions."[29]

I am less sanguine than Pinnock about the current state of evangelicalism. Perhaps both of us assess the situation from a jaundiced viewpoint, suffering from the "grass is always greener" syndrome. Pinnock indicates that one purpose of *The Grace of God, the Will of Man* is to "give a louder voice to the silent majority of Arminian evangelicals."[30] Here he avers that the evangelical masses are departing from the hold Augustinian thinking has had on them. He says, "It is hard to find a Calvinistic theologian willing to defend Reformed theology, including the views of both Calvin and Luther, in all its rigorous particulars now that Gordon H. Clark is no longer with us and John Gerstner is retired. Few have the stomach to tolerate Calvinian theology in its logical purity."[31]

Since these words were penned, Dr. Gerstner has died, so perhaps we need the lamp of Diogenes to find Calvinistic theologians who will defend both Luther and Calvin with rigor. The news of the demise of Calvinism is a bit exaggerated, however, as there remain many with theological stomachs of cast iron.

In his own pilgrimage Pinnock came to question God's omniscience and foreknowledge. He understands the pivotal relationship between these divine attributes and the doctrines of election and free will. He writes:

Finally I had to rethink the divine omniscience and reluctantly ask whether we ought to think of it as an exhaustive foreknowledge of everything that will ever happen, as even most Arminians do. I found I could not shake off the intuition that such a total omniscience would necessarily mean that everything we will ever choose in the future will have been already spelled out in the divine knowledge register, and consequently the belief that we have truly significant choices to make would seem to be mistaken. I knew the Calvinist argument that exhaustive foreknowledge was tantamount to predestination because it implies the fixity of all things from "eternity past," and I could not shake off its logical force.[32]

It is important to note that Pinnock's new view of God's foreknowledge goes beyond that of most Arminians, as he indicates. It appears to go well beyond the views espoused in the middle-knowledge concept developed by the Spanish Jesuit Luis Molina. This concept is ably expounded by William Lane Craig in *The Grace of God, the Will of Man*,[33] and also lucidly developed by Alvin Plantinga. Pinnock seeks to escape the "logic" of exhaustive foreknowledge in classical Reformed theology. He says:

> Therefore, I had to ask myself if it was biblically possible to hold that God knows everything that can be known, but that free choices would not be something that can be known even by God because they are not yet settled in reality. . . . God can predict a great deal of what we will choose to do, but not all of it, because some of it remains hidden in the mystery of human freedom. . . .
> . . . Of course the Bible praises God for his detailed knowledge of what will happen and what he himself will do. . . . The God of the Bible displays an openness to the future that the traditional view of omniscience simply cannot accommodate. . . .
> . . . We need a "free will" theism, a doctrine of God that treads the middle path between classical theism, which exaggerates God's transcendence of the world, and process theism, which presses for radical immanence.[34]

This statement expresses some of Pinnock's seminal thinking, which he develops more fully in the later volume *The Openness of God*. What is noteworthy here is that Pinnock clearly realizes that he is challenging, not merely classical Calvinism, but classical theism itself. He seeks to reconstruct theology somewhere between classical theism and process theology. He calls it "free-will theism" because the driving force behind this new doctrine of God is the concern to maintain the Arminian view of human free will. In *The Openness of God* Pinnock reiterates his critique of the doctrine of omniscience in classical theism and also raises questions about other doctrines of classical theism, such as immutability and omnipotence.[35]

On the surface this reconstruction of the doctrine of God appears to carry a heavy price tag if it achieves the openness Pinnock desires. At the practical level we wonder how God can know anything about the future except what he personally intends to do (intentions that are themselves open to change as he reacts to future decisions of men). If history is affected at all by the decisions of men and if God's knowledge does not include future human decisions, how can God know anything about the future of world history? How can we find any comfort in the future God has promised for his people if that future destiny rests in the hands of men? The anchor of our souls has been set adrift from its moorings. We have no reason to trust in any promise God has made about the future. Not only may the best laid plans of mice and men go astray, but the best laid plans of the Creator of mice and men may likewise go astray.

This fascination with the openness of God is an assault not merely on Calvinism, or even on classical theism, but on Christianity itself.

If the case be such indeed,
that all mankind are by nature
in a state of total ruin, . . .
then, doubtless,
the great salvation by Christ
stands in direct relation
to this ruin,
as the remedy to the disease.

Jonathan Edwards

7

We Are Inclined to Sin:
Jonathan Edwards

part from his famous sermon, *Sinners in the Hands of an Angry God*, Jonathan Edwards is most known for his twin works *Religious Affections* (1746) and *Freedom of the Will* (1754). One of his lesser known works is on original sin, an important work published posthumously.

In *The Great Christian Doctrine of Original Sin Defended* (1758), Edwards was not replying to any specific author, but he was moved to write what he called a "general defence" of this important doctrine. He says of it in his preface: "I look on the doctrine as of *great importance;* which every body will doubtless own it is, if it be *true.* For, if the case be such indeed, that all mankind are by *nature* in a state of *total ruin,* both with respect to the *moral evil* of which they are the subjects, and the *afflictive evil* to which they are exposed, the one as the consequence and punishment of the other; then, doubtless, the great *salvation* by CHRIST stands in direct relation to this *ruin,* as the remedy to the disease; and the whole *gospel,* or doctrine of salvation, must *suppose* it; and all real belief, or true notion of that gospel, must be built upon it."[1]

Much of the controversy over human free will is waged in the context of speculative debate over the relationship of man's freedom to God's knowledge, or to election and reprobation. For Edwards the central issue of free will is rooted in the ancient controversy (as between Pelagius and Augustine) over the relationship of free will to man's fallen nature and ultimately to his redemption through the gospel. In a word, Edwards focuses on the broader issue of biblical redemption or the gospel. This same motive drove Martin Luther in his debate with Erasmus: the concern to see *sola fide* solidly rooted in *sola gratia.* For Edwards, the greatness of the gospel is visible only when viewed against the backdrop of the greatness of the ruin into which we have been plunged by the fall. The greatness of the disease requires the greatness of the remedy.

Evidence for Original Sin

One interesting facet of Edwards's defense of the classical view of the fall and original sin is his attempt to show that, even if the Bible were silent on the matter, this doctrine would be demonstrated by the evidence of natural reason. Since the phenomena of human history demonstrate that sin is a universal reality, we should seek an explanation for this reality. In simple terms the question is, Why do all people sin?

Those who deny the doctrine of original sin usually answer this question by pointing to the corrupting influences of decadent societies. Man is born in a state of innocence, they say, but he is subsequently corrupted by the immoral influence of society. This idea begs the question, How did society become corrupt in the first place? If all people are born innocent or in a state of moral neutrality, with no predisposition to sin, why do not at least a statistical average of 50% of the people remain innocent? Why can we find no societies in which the prevailing influence is to virtue rather than vice? Why does not society influence us to maintain our natural innocence?

Even the most sanguine critics of human nature, those who insist that man is basically good, repeat the persistent axiomatic aphorism "Nobody's perfect." Why is no one perfect? If man is good at the core of his heart and evil is peripheral, tangential, or accidental, why does not the core win out over the tangent, the substance over the accidents? Even in the society in which we find ourselves today, in which moral absolutes are widely denied,

<table>

Events in the Life of Edwards	
1703	Born in East Windsor, Conn.
1716–20	Studied at Yale
1726	Became assistant minister in Northampton, Mass.
1727	Married Sarah Pierrepont
1729	Became minister in Northampton
1734	Great Awakening began in Northampton
1751	Moved to Stockbridge to be pastor, missionary
1758	Inaugurated president of Princeton
	Died in Princeton, N.J.

people still readily admit that no one is perfect. The concept of "perfect" has been denuded by the rejection of moral absolutes. Yet with a lower standard or norm of perfection than the one revealed by Scripture, we recognize that even this "norm" is not met. With the lowest common denominator of ethics such as Immanuel Kant's categorical imperative, we still face the frustration of failing to live up to it.

We may discount ethical standards, reducing them below the level of actual perfection, and still fail to meet those standards. People claim a commitment to moral relativism, but when somebody steals our purse or our wallet, we still cry, "Foul." Suddenly the credo that "everyone has the right to do his own thing" is challenged when the other person's "thing" conflicts with my "thing."

Edwards saw in the universal reality of sin manifold evidence for a universal *tendency* toward sin. Edwards states an objection to this and then answers the objection:

> If any should say, Though it be evident that there is a tendency in the state of things to this general event—that all mankind should

fail of perfect obedience, and should sin, and incur a demerit of eternal ruin; and also that this tendency does not lie in any distinguishing circumstances of any particular people, person, or age—yet it may not lie in *man's nature,* but in the general constitution and frame of *this world.* Though the nature of man may be good, without any evil propensity inherent in it; yet the nature and universal state of this world may be full of so many and strong temptations, and of such powerful influence on such a creature as man, dwelling in so infirm a body, etc. that the result of the whole may be a strong and infallible tendency *in such a state of things,* to the sin and eternal ruin of every one of mankind.[2]

Edwards answers this supposition with the following reply:

To this I would reply, that such an evasion will not at all avail to the purpose of those whom I oppose in this controversy. It alters not the case as to this question, Whether man, in his present state, is depraved and ruined by propensities to sin. If any creature be of such a nature that it proves evil in its proper place, or in the situation which God has assigned it in the universe, it is of an evil nature. That part of the system is not good, which is not good in its place in the system; and those inherent qualities of that part of the system, which are not good, but corrupt, in that place, are justly looked upon as evil inherent qualities. That propensity is truly esteemed to belong to the *nature* of any being, or to be inherent in it, that is the necessary consequence of its nature, considered together with its proper situation in the universal system of existence, whether that propensity be good or bad.[3]

Edwards draws an analogy from nature to illustrate his point: "It is the *nature* of a stone to be heavy; but yet, if it were placed, as it might be, at a distance from this world, it would have no such quality. But being a stone, is of such a nature, that it will have this quality or tendency, in its proper place, in this world, where God has made it, it is properly looked upon as a propensity belonging to its nature. . . . So, if mankind are of such a nature, that they have an universal effectual tendency to sin and ruin in this world, where God has made and placed them, this is to be looked upon as a pernicious tendency belonging to their nature."[4]

Edwards concludes that within the nature of man there is a propensity toward sin. This inclination is part of the inherent or constituent nature of man. It is natural to fallen mankind. When Scripture speaks of "natural man," it refers to man as he is since the fall, not as he was created originally. The fall was a real fall and not a maintenance of the status quo of creation.

John Calvin acknowledged that men, though fallen, perform works of seeming righteousness, and he called these works acts of *civic righteousness.* Such "virtues," which Augustine called "splendid vices," may conform outwardly to the law of God, but they do not proceed from a heart inclined to please God, or from a heart that loves God. In biblical categories a good or virtuous work must not only conform outwardly to the prescriptions of God's law but also proceed from an inward disposition or motive rooted in the love of God. In a real sense the Great Commandment to love God with all the heart underlies the moral judgment of all human activity.

Concerning the *preponderance* of evil deeds over good ones, Edwards says: "Let never so many thousands or millions of acts of honesty, good nature, etc. be supposed; yet, by the supposition, there is an unfailing propensity to such moral evil, as in its dreadful consequences infinitely outweighs all effects or consequences of any supposed good."[5]

Edwards goes on to point out the degree of wickedness and heinousness that is involved in merely one sin against God. Such an act would be so wicked since it is committed against such a holy being that it would outweigh the sum of any amount of contrasting virtue. "He that in any respect or degree is a transgressor of God's law," Edwards says, "is a wicked man, yea, wholly wicked in the eye of the law; all his goodness being esteemed nothing, having no account made of it, when taken together with his wickedness."[6]

At this point Edwards echoes the sentiment of James, saying that to sin against one point of the law is to sin against the whole law (James 2:10–11) and, of course, the Law-Giver himself. Likewise, Edwards says works of obedience, strictly speaking, cannot outweigh disobedience. When we are obedient, we are merely doing what God requires us to do. Here we can be nothing more than unprofitable servants.

Edwards sees evidence for man's depraved nature in the propensity of humans to sin immediately, as soon as they are morally capable of committing actual sin. He sees further evidence in the fact that man sins continually and progressively, and that the tendency remains even in the most sanctified of men. Edwards also finds significant what he calls the "extreme degree of folly and stupidity in matters of religion."[7]

In a cursory look at human history, Edwards provides a catalogue of woes and calamities that have been perpetrated by and on the human race. Even the most jaded observer of history must admit that things are not right with the world. Then Edwards turns to the universality of death as proof for the universality of sin. In the biblical view, death came into the world through and because of sin. It represents the divine judgment on human wickedness, a judgment visited even on babies who die in infancy. "Death is spoken of in Scripture as the *chief* of calamities," Edwards notes, "the most extreme and terrible of all natural evils in this world."[8]

The Bible and Original Sin

Edwards then turns his attention to the scriptural warrant for the doctrine of original sin. He pays particular attention to Paul's teaching in Ephesians 2.

Another passage of the apostle, to the like purpose with that which we have been considering in the 5th [chapter] of Romans, is that in Ephesians 2:3—"And were by nature children of wrath, even as others." This remains a plain testimony to the doctrine of original sin, as held by those who used to be called orthodox Christians, after all the pains and art used to torture and pervert it. This doctrine is here not only plainly and fully taught, but abundantly so, if we take the words with the context; where Christians are once and again represented as being, in their first state, *dead in sin,* and as *quickened* and *raised up* from such a state of death, in a most marvellous display of free *rich grace and love,* and *exceeding greatness of God's power, etc.*[9]

With respect to the uniform teaching of Scripture, Edwards concludes: "As this place in general is very full and plain, so the doctrine of the corruption of nature, as derived from Adam, and also the imputation of his first sin, are *both* clearly taught in it. The *imputation* of *Adam's* one transgression, is indeed most directly and frequently asserted. We are here assured, that 'by one man's sin, death passed on all.' . . . And it is repeated, over and over, that 'all are condemned,' 'many are dead,' 'many made sinners,' etc. 'by one man's offence,' 'by the disobedience of one,' and 'by one offence.'"[10]

Finally Edwards argues for original sin from the biblical teaching regarding the application of redemption. The Spirit's work in regeneration is a necessary antidote for a previous, corrupt condition: "It is almost needless to observe, how evidently this is spoken of as *necessary* to salvation, and as the change in which are attained the habits of true virtue and holiness, and the character of a true saint; as has been observed of *regeneration, conversion, etc.* and how apparent it is, that the change is the *same.* . . . So that all these phrases imply, having a *new heart,* and being *renewed in the spirit,* according to their plain signification."[11]

In his introduction to the Yale edition of Edwards's *Freedom of the Will,* Paul Ramsey makes this observation:

> Into the writing of it he poured all his intellectual acumen, coupled with a passionate conviction that the decay to be observed in religion and morals followed the decline in doctrine since the founding of New England. The jeremiads, he believed, had better go to the bottom of the religious issue! The product of such plain

---

Related Works by Edwards

The Great Christian Doctrine of Original Sin Defended: Evidences of Its Truth Produced, and Arguments to the Contrary Answered . . . In *The Works of Jonathan Edwards, A.M.* 10th ed. 2 vols. 1865. Reprint. Edinburgh / Carlisle, Penn.: Banner of Truth, 1979. 1:143–233.

Freedom of the Will. Edited by Paul Ramsey. The Works of Jonathan Edwards, edited by Perry Miller, vol. 1. New Haven and London: Yale University, 1957.

A Jonathan Edwards Reader. Edited by John E. Smith, Harry S. Stout, and Kenneth P. Minkema. New Haven: Yale University, 1995.

living, high thinking, funded experience and such vital passion was the present *Inquiry,* a superdreadnaught which Edwards sent forth to combat contingency and self-determination (to reword [David F.] Swenson's praise of one of [Søren] Kierkegaard's big books) and in which he delivered the most thoroughgoing and absolutely destructive criticism that liberty of indifference, without necessity, has ever received. This has to be said even if one is persuaded that some form of the viewpoint Edwards opposed still has whereon to stand. This book alone is sufficient to establish its author as the greatest philosopher-theologian yet to grace the American scene.[12]

In his own preface to *Freedom of the Will,* Edwards speaks of the danger of pinning labels on representatives of various schools of theological thought and the needless rancor often attached to such labels. Yet he pleads that generic terms are necessary for the sake of literary smoothness. A writer must have a shorthand way of distinguishing various characteristics of systems of thought. Although he does not agree with Calvin at every point, Edwards says he is not offended when labeled a *Calvinist* because he stands so squarely in that tradition.

His chief concern, however, is that the reader understand the consequences of differing theological perspectives. He regards the question of human freedom with the same earnestness Luther displayed in his debate with Erasmus. Far from being an isolated, peripheral, speculative matter, Edwards thinks this question is supremely important. He says:

> The subject is of such importance, as to *demand* attention, and the most thorough consideration. Of all kinds of knowledge that we can ever obtain, the knowledge of God, and the knowledge of ourselves, are the most important. As religion is the great business, for which we are created, and on which our happiness depends; and as religion consists in an intercourse between ourselves and our Maker; and so has its foundation in God's nature and ours, and in the relation that God and we stand in to each other; therefore a true knowledge of both must be needful in order to true religion. But the knowledge of ourselves consists chiefly in right apprehensions concerning those two chief faculties of our

nature, the *understanding* and *will.* Both are very important: yet the science of the latter must be confessed to be of greatest moment; inasmuch as all virtue and religion have their seat more immediately in the will, consisting more especially in right acts and habits of this faculty. And the grand question about the freedom of the will, is the main point that belongs to the science of the will. Therefore I say, the importance of this subject greatly *demands* the attention of Christians, and especially of divines.[13]

Why We Choose

Edwards begins his inquiry by defining the will as "the mind choosing." ". . . the will (without any metaphysical refining) is plainly, that by which the mind chooses anything," he writes. "The faculty of the will is that faculty or power or principle of mind by which it is capable of choosing: an act of the will is the same as an act of choosing or choice."[14]

Even when a person does not choose a given option, the mind is choosing "the absence of the thing refused."[15] Edwards called these choices voluntary or "elective" actions.

John Locke asserted that "the will is perfectly distinguished from desire." Edwards argues that will and desire are not "so entirely distinct, that they can ever be properly said to run counter. A man never, in any instance, wills anything contrary to his desires, or desires anything contrary to his will."[16]

This brief assertion is critical to understanding Edwards's view of the will. He maintains that a man *never* chooses contrary to his desire. This means that man *always* acts according to his desire. Edwards indicates that the determining factor in every choice is the "strongest motive" present at that moment. In summary, we always choose according to the strongest motive or desire at the time.

People may debate this point with Edwards, recalling moments when they chose something they really did not want to choose. To understand Edwards, we must consider the complexities involved in making choices. Our desires are often complex and even in conflict with each other. Even the Apostle Paul experienced conflicting desires, claiming that what he wanted to do he failed to do and what he did not want to do he actually did (see Rom. 7:15). Does the apostle here belie Edwards's point? I think not. Paul expresses the struggle he endures between desires in conflict. When he chooses what he "does not want to choose," he is experiencing what I call the "all things being equal" dimension.

For example, every Christian has some desire in his heart to be righteous. All things being equal, we want always to be righteous. Yet a war is going on inside of us because we also continue to have wicked desires. When we choose the wicked over the righteous course of action, at that moment we desire the sin more than obedience to God. That was as true for Paul as it is for us. Every time we sin we desire more to do that than we do to obey Christ. Otherwise we simply would not sin.

Not only are desires not monolithic, but also they are not constant in their force or intensity. Our desire levels fluctuate from moment to moment. For example, the dieter desires to lose weight. After a full meal it is easy to say no to sweets. The appetite has been sated and the desire for more food diminished. As time passes, however, and self-denial has led to an increased hunger, the desire for food intensifies. The desire to lose weight remains. But when the desire to gorge oneself becomes stronger than the desire to lose weight, the dieter's resolve weakens and he succumbs to temptation. All things do not remain in a constant state of equality.

Another example is a person being robbed. The robber points a gun at the person and says, "Your money or your life!" (We remember the skit made famous by Jack Benny. When posed with this option, Benny hesitated for a protracted time. In frustration the robber said, "What are you waiting for?" Benny replied, "I'm thinking it over.") To be robbed at gunpoint is to experience a form of external coercion. The coercion reduces the person's options to two. All things being equal, the person has no desire to donate the contents of his wallet to the thief. But with only two options the person will respond according to his strongest motive at the moment. He may conclude that if he refuses to hand over his wallet, the robber will both kill him and take his money. Most people will opt to hand the money over because they desire to live more than they desire to keep their wallets. It is possible, however, that a person has such a strong antipathy to armed robbery that he would prefer to die rather than give over his wallet "willingly."

Because this example contains a coercive dimension, I put the word *willingly* in quotation marks. We must ask if under these circumstances the action really is voluntary? It is if we view it in the context of only two options. However much external coercion is involved, there still remains a choice. Even here, Edwards would say, the person will choose the alternative for which he or she has the stronger motive.

The strongest-motive concept may be lost on us when we consider the manifold decisions we make every day without thoroughly considering the options available to us. We walk into a classroom where several seats are vacant or we walk to an unoccupied park bench and sit down. Rarely do we list the pros and cons before selecting a seat or a part of the bench. On the surface it seems that these choices are entirely arbitrary. We choose them without thinking. If that is so, it belies Edwards's thesis that the will is the "mind choosing."

Such choices seem to be mindless ones, but if we analyze them closely, we discover that some preference or motive is operating, albeit subtly. The motive factors may be so slight that they escape our notice. Experiments have been run in which people choose a seat on an unoccupied park bench. Some people always sit in the middle of the bench. Some are gregarious and long for company, so they choose the middle of the bench in hopes that someone will come along and sit beside them. And some people pre-

Related Works about Edwards

Gerstner, John H. *The Rational Biblical Theology of Jonathan Edwards.* 3 vols. Powhatan, Va.: Berea / Orlando: Ligonier, 1991–93.

Gerstner, John H. *Jonathan Edwards: A Mini-Theology.* Wheaton: Tyndale, 1987.

Lang, J. Stephen, ed. *Jonathan Edwards and the Great Awakening. Christian History* 4, 4 (1985).

Murray, Iain H. *Jonathan Edwards: A New Biography.* Edinburgh and Carlisle, Penn.: Banner of Truth, 1987.

fer solitude, so they sit in the middle in hopes that no one else will sit on the bench.

Likewise some people prefer to sit in the front of the classroom or the back for various reasons. The decision to select a certain seat is not an involuntary action like the beating of one's heart. It is a voluntary action, which proceeds from some motive, however slight or obscure. In a word, there is a *reason* why we choose the seats we choose.

What Determines Our Choices

In his analysis of choices, Edwards discusses the determination of the will. He writes: "By 'determining the will,' if the phrase be used with any meaning, must be intended, causing that the act of the will or choice should be thus, and not otherwise: and the will is said to be determined, when, in consequence of some action, or influence, its choice is directed to, and fixed upon a particular object."[17]

Edwards is not speaking of what is commonly called *determinism*, the idea that human actions are determined by some form of external coercion such as fate or manifest destiny. Rather he is here speaking of *self-determination*, which is the essence of human volition.

Edwards considers utterly irrational the idea that an "indifferent will" makes choices. "To talk of the determination of the will, supposes an effect, which must have a cause," he says. "If the will be determined, there is a determiner. This must be supposed to be intended even by them that say, the will determines itself. If it be so, the will is both determiner and determined; it is a cause that acts and produces effects upon itself, and is the object of its own influence and action."[18]

At this point Edwards argues from the vantage point of the law of cause and effect. Causality is presupposed throughout his argument. The law of cause and effect declares that for every effect there is an antecedent cause. Every effect must have a cause and every cause, in order to be a cause, must produce an effect. The law of causality is a formal principle that one cannot deny without embracing irrationality. David Hume's famous critique of causality did not annihilate the law but our ability to *perceive* particular causal relationships.

The law of causality with which Edwards operates is "formal" in that it has no material content in itself and is stated in such a way as to be analytically true. That is, it is true by analysis of its terms or "by definition." In this regard the law of causality is merely an extension of the law of noncontradiction. An *effect*, by definition, is that which has an antecedent cause. If it has no cause then it is not an effect. Likewise, a *cause* by definition is that which produces an effect. If no effect is produced then it is not a cause.

I once was criticized in a journal article by a scholar who complained, "The problem with Sproul is that he doesn't allow for an uncaused effect." I plead guilty to the charge, but I see this as virtue rather than vice. People who allow for uncaused effects are allowing for irrational nonsense statements to be true. If Sproul is guilty here, Edwards is more so. Edwards is far more cogent in his critical analysis of the intricacies of causality than Sproul will ever be in this life.

When Edwards declares that the will is both determined and determiner, he is not indulging in contradiction. The will is not determined and the determiner at the same time and in the same relationship. The will is the determiner in one sense and is determined in another sense. It is the determiner in the sense that it produces the effects of real choices. It is determined in the sense that those choices are caused by the motive that is the strongest one in the mind at the moment of choosing.

John H. Gerstner, perhaps the twentieth century's greatest expert on Edwards, writes:

> Edwards understands the soul to have two parts: understanding and will. Not only is *Freedom of the Will* based on this dichotomy; that dichotomy underlies *Religious Affections* as well. . . .
>
> Edwards agreed with the English Puritan, John Preston, that the mind came first and the heart or will second. "Such is the nature

of man, that no object can come at the heart but through the door of the understanding. . . ." In the garden, man *could have* rejected the temptation of the mind to move the will to disobey God. After the fall he could not, although Arminians and Pelagians thought otherwise. Their notion of the "freedom of the will" made it always possible for the will to reject what the mind presented. This perverted notion, Edwards said in *Original Sin,* "seems to be a grand favorite point with Pelagians and Arminians, and all divines of such characters, in their controversies with the orthodox." For Edwards, acts of the will are not free in the sense of uncaused.[19]

To Edwards a motive is "something that is extant in the view or apprehension of the understanding, or perceiving faculty."[20] He says:

> . . . Nothing can induce or invite the mind to will or act anything, any further than it is perceived, or is some way or other in the mind's view; for what is wholly unperceived, and perfectly out of the mind's view, can't affect the mind at all. . . .
> . . . everything that is properly called a motive, excitement or inducement to a perceiving willing agent, has some sort and degree of tendency, or advantage to move or excite the will, previous to the effect, or to the act of the will excited. This previous tendency of the motive is what I call the "strength" of the motive. . . . that which appears most inviting, and has, by what appears concerning it to the understanding or apprehension, the greatest degree of previous tendency to excite and induce the choice, is what I call the "strongest motive." And in this sense, I suppose the will is always determined by the strongest motive.[21]

Edwards further argues that the strongest motive is that which appears most "good" or "pleasing" to the mind. Here he uses *good* not in the moral sense, because we may be most pleased by doing what is not good morally. Rather the volition acts according to that which appears most agreeable to the person. That which is most pleasing may be deemed as pleasure. What entices fallen man to sin is the desire for some perceived pleasure.

Edwards then turns his attention to the terms *necessity* and *contingency.* He says "that a thing is . . . said to be necessary, when it must be, and cannot be otherwise."[22] He goes beyond the ordinary use of the word *necessary* to the philosophical use. He says:

> Philosophical necessity is really nothing else than the full and fixed connection between the things signified by the subject and predicate of a proposition, which affirms something to be true. When there is such a connection, then the thing affirmed in the proposition is necessary, in a philosophical sense; whether any opposition, or contrary effort be supposed, or supposable in the case, or no. When the subject and predicate of the proposition, which affirms the existence of anything, either substance, quality, act or circumstance, have a full and certain connection, then the existence or being of that thing is said to be necessary in a metaphysical sense. And in this sense I use the word *necessity,* in the following discourse, when I endeavor to prove that necessity is not inconsistent with liberty.[23]

Edwards discusses various types of necessary connection. He observes that one type of connection is *consequential:* "things which are perfectly connected with other things that are necessary, are necessary themselves, by a necessity of consequence."[24] This is to say that if A is necessary and B is perfectly connected to A, then B is also necessary. It is only by such necessity of consequence that Edwards speaks of future necessities. Such future necessities are *necessary* in this way alone.

Similarly Edwards considers the term *contingent.* There is a difference between how the word is used in ordinary language and how it functions in philosophical discourse. He writes:

> . . . Anything is said to be contingent, or to come to pass by chance or accident, in the original meaning of such words, when its connection with its causes or antecedents, according to the established course of things, is not discerned; and so is what we have no means of the foresight of. And especially is anything said to be contingent or accidental with regard to us, when anything comes to pass that we are concerned in, as occasions or subjects, without our foreknowledge, and beside our design and scope.
>
> But the word *contingent* is abundantly used in a very different sense; not for that whose connection with the series of things we

can't discern, so as to foresee the event; but for something which has absolutely no previous ground or reason, with which its existence has any fixed and certain connection.[25]

In ordinary language we attribute to accident or "chance" any unintended consequences. In a technical sense nothing occurs by chance, for chance has no being and can exercise no power. When the term *contingent* refers to effects with no ground or reason, it retreats to the assertion that there are effects without causes. It is one thing to say that we do not know what causes a given effect; it is quite another thing to say that nothing causes the effect. Nothing cannot do anything because it is not anything.[26]

Our Moral Inability

One of the most important distinctions made by Edwards is the one between natural ability and moral ability. He also distinguishes between natural necessity and moral necessity. *Natural necessity* refers to those things that occur via natural force. *Moral necessity* refers to those effects that result from moral causes such as the strength of inclination or motive. He applies these distinctions to the issue of moral *inability*.

We are said to be *naturally* unable to do a thing, when we can't do it if we will, because what is most commonly called nature [doesn't] allow . . . it, or because of some impeding defect or obstacle that is extrinsic to the will; either in the faculty of understanding, constitution of body, or external objects. *Moral* inability consists not in any of these things; but either in the want of inclination; or the strength of a contrary inclination; or the want of sufficient motives in view, to induce and excite the act of the will, or the strength of apparent motives to the contrary. Or both these may be resolved into one; and it may be said in one word, that moral inability consists in the opposition or want of inclination.[27]

Man may have the desire to do things he cannot do because of limits imposed by nature. We may wish to be Superman, able to leap tall buildings in a single bound, more powerful than a locomotive, and faster than a speeding bullet. But unless we become fifteen–million-dollar men (up from six million due to inflation), it is highly unlikely that we will ever perform such prodigious feats. Nature enables birds to fly through the air without the aid of mechanical devices, and fish to live under-water without drowning. They are so constituted in their natures to be able to do these things. But we lack wings and feathers, or gills and fins. These are limitations imposed by nature. They reveal a lack or deficiency of necessary faculties or equipment.

Moral inability also deals with a deficiency, the lack of sufficient motive or inclination. Edwards cites various examples of moral inability: an honorable woman who is morally unable to be a prostitute, a loving child who is unwilling to kill his father, a lascivious man who cannot rein in his lust.

Given man's moral inability, the will cannot not be free. The will is always free to act according to the strongest motive or inclination at the moment. For Edwards, this is the essence of freedom. To be able to choose what one desires is to be free in this sense. When I say the will cannot not be free, I mean the will cannot choose against its strongest inclination. It cannot choose what it does not desire to choose. Edwards refers to the common meaning of *liberty:* "... that power and opportunity for one to do and conduct as he will, or according to his choice." The word says nothing of "the cause or original of that choice."[28]

Edwards notes that Arminians and Pelagians have a different meaning for the term *liberty*. He lists a few aspects of their definition:

1. It consists in a self-determining power or a certain sovereignty the will has over itself, whereby it determines its own volitions.
2. Indifference belongs to liberty previous to the act of volition, *in equilibrio*.
3. Contingence belongs to liberty and is essential to it. Unless the will is free in this sense, it is deemed to be not free at all.[29]

Edwards then shows that the Pelagian notion is irrational and leads to an infinite regress of determination:

> . . . If the will determines the will, then choice orders and determines the choice: and acts of choice are subject to the decision, and follow the conduct of other acts of choice. And therefore if the will determines all its own free acts, then every free act of choice is determined by a preceding act of choice, choosing that act. And if that preceding act of the will or choice be also a free act, then by these principles, in this act too, the will is self-determined; that is, this, in like manner, is an act that the soul voluntarily chooses. . . . Which brings us directly to a contradiction: for it supposes an act of the will preceding the first act in the whole train, directing and determining the rest; or a free act of the will, before the first free act of the will. Or else we must come at last to an act of the will, determining the consequent acts, wherein the will is not self-determined, and so is not a free act . . . but if the first act in the train . . . be not free, none of them all can be free. . . .
> . . . if the first is not determined by the will, and so not free, then none of them are truly determined by the will. . . .[30]

Edwards says the idea of an indifferent will is absurd. First, if the will functions from a standpoint of indifference, having no motive or inclination, then how can the choice be a moral one? If decisions are utterly arbitrary and done for no reason or motive, how do they differ from involuntary actions, or from the mere responses of plants, animals, or falling bodies?

Second, if the will is indifferent, how can there be a choice at all? If there is no motive or inclination, how can a choice be made? It requires an effect without a cause. For this reason, Edwards labors the question of whether volition can possibly arise without a cause through the activity of the nature of the soul. For Edwards it is axiomatic that "nothing has no choice."[31] "Choice or preference can't be before itself, in the same instance, either in the order of time or nature," he says. "It can't be the foundation of itself, or the fruit or consequence of itself."[32]

Here Edwards applies the law of noncontradiction to the Pelagian and Arminian view of free will, and he shows that it is absurd. Indifference can only suspend choices, not create them. To create them would be to act *ex nihilo,* not only without a material cause, but also without a sufficient or efficient cause.

Edwards then treats several common objections to the Augustinian view, but we will not deal with them here. We conclude by summarizing Edwards's view of original sin. Man is morally incapable of choosing the things of God unless or until God changes the disposition of his soul. Man's moral inability is due to a critical lack and deficiency, namely the motive or desire for the things of God. Left to himself, man will never choose Christ. He has no inclination to do so in his fallen state. Since he cannot act against his strongest inclination, he will never choose Christ unless God first changes the inclination of his soul by the immediate and supernatural work of regeneration. Only God can liberate the sinner from his bondage to his own evil inclinations.

Like Augustine, Luther, and Calvin, Edwards argues that man is free in that he can and does choose what he desires or is inclined to choose. But man lacks the desire for Christ and the things of God until God creates in his soul a positive inclination for these things.

If the nature is sinful,
in such a sense that action
must necessarily be sinful, . . .
then sin in action
must be a calamity,
and can be no crime. . . .
 This cannot be a crime,
since the will has nothing
to do with it.

Charles Grandison Finney

We Are Not Depraved by Nature:
Charles Grandison Finney

C harles Grandison Finney is a hero to the contemporary evangelical community. The front cover of the 1994 edition of Finney's *Systematic Theology*[1] heralds him as "America's Greatest Revivalist." The back cover credits Finney with directly or indirectly being responsible for the conversions of around 500,000 people. In like manner Charles White's review of Keith J. Hardman's 1987 biography of Finney hails him as "the premier evangelist of the nineteenth century."[2]

Finney's influence on subsequent generations of evangelists is a matter of record. In the preface to his biography Hardman writes: "Many questions surround a study of Charles Finney. He has often been regarded as the initiator of modern mass evangelism. He supposedly developed innovative methods to bring about more conversions, a new style of preaching to audiences, and from these the entire attitude toward evangelism was transformed. Stemming from Charles G. Finney, some have held, are all the techniques and attitudes of modern large-scale evangelism: Dwight L. Moody, J. Wilbur Chapman, Billy Sunday, and Billy Graham carried the attitudes forward virtually unchanged, and modified the techniques only as later times demanded."[3]

As revered and esteemed as Finney is, he was not without his critics in the nineteenth century. Perhaps chief among them was the Princeton theologian Charles Hodge. *Finney's Systematic Theology* includes an appendix by George F. Wright of Andover, Massachusetts, in which Wright complains that Hodge grossly misunderstood and misrepresented Finney.

Perhaps to undertake a modern criticism of Finney is to evoke the wrath of the evangelical community and is at best a fool's errand. But others have dared to tread this path. In an essay in *Modern Reformation,* Robert Godfrey, president of Westminster Theological Seminary in Escondido, California, writes: ". . . the wonderful thing about Finney is that he is so clear. I make my students read a big chunk of Finney at seminary because I've always believed that if I tried to summarize him, they wouldn't believe that I was being fair. Because, in the whole history of the church there is probably not a theologian as Pelagian as Finney. Finney begins to make Pelagius look good. And Finney's great insight, made perfectly clear on the first few pages of his *Lectures on Revival,* is that conversion comes about by the exercise of free will."[4]

Later in the same article Godfrey says: "B. B. Warfield once observed of the theology of Charles Finney: 'God might be eliminated from it entirely without essentially changing its character.' The same might be said of contemporary evangelicalism. We need sharper analysis and pointed refutation."[5]

Godfrey's criticism is only slightly more severe than Warfield's when, as a historian, he charges that in all of church history "there is probably not a theologian as Pelagian as Finney."

In the introduction to *Finney's Systematic Theology,* L. G. Parkhurst Jr. says of Finney: "He tried to be Biblical, rather than adhere to any theological system or group of his day. In some cases, he seems to take a middle ground between the old school

Calvinists and Arminians, which makes each group critical of certain parts of his theology."[6] Earlier Parkhurst says, "Those less informed in matters of sound theology have promoted and passed on to others the falsehood that Finney was not orthodox in his theology or that his gospel was not according to the gospel of Paul."[7]

<table>
<tr><th colspan="2">Events in the Life of Finney</th></tr>
<tr><td>1792</td><td>Born in Warren, Conn.</td></tr>
<tr><td>1818</td><td>Entered field of law</td></tr>
<tr><td>1821</td><td>Converted to Christianity</td></tr>
<tr><td>1824</td><td>Ordained to the ministry
Married Lydia Root</td></tr>
<tr><td>1843–44</td><td>Experienced "second blessing"</td></tr>
<tr><td>1846–47</td><td>Published vols. 2–3 of *Systematic Theology*</td></tr>
<tr><td>1851</td><td>Elected president of Oberlin College</td></tr>
<tr><td>1875</td><td>Died in Oberlin, Ohio</td></tr>
</table>

I find it difficult to perceive how Finney fits *between* Calvinism and Arminianism. The debate between these two schools seems more reminiscent of the debate between Augustinianism and semi-Pelagianism. If Finney was Pelagian (as Godfrey asserts), then he is outside the scope of both Calvinism and Arminianism. Parkhurst says those who have questioned Finney's orthodoxy are uninformed in sound theology. Perhaps that is true of Hodge, Warfield, and Godfrey, and perhaps for me as well, but it is difficult to find in Finney much that is theologically orthodox.

First we must ask if Finney was an evangelical. In one sense this question is easy to answer, but in another sense it is most difficult. The difficulty lies in defining the term *evangelical*. Before we can assess if someone is evangelical, we must understand what the label means.

All words, but particularly labels, go through changes of nuance and meaning. Lexicographers routinely note the shift in the meaning of words from their original derivation to contemporary usage. We see this shift clearly with the term *fundamentalist*. This word was originally coined in an academic debate over the foundational doctrines of historic Christianity. Today it is often applied to those who are anti-intellectual and moralistic in their faith. In similar manner there is a crisis over the meaning of the term *evangelical*.

Historically the term *evangelical* was a virtual synonym for *Protestant.* It was linked to the Protestant Reformation and referred particularly to the pivotal doctrine of *sola fide,* or justification by faith alone. The magisterial Reformers believed that this doctrine rescued the biblical gospel or "evangel" from Roman distortions. For centuries, though divided on a host of theological issues, evangelicalism shared a commitment to *sola fide.*

Today agreement even on this point is rapidly disintegrating, as evidenced by the dispute over the nature of the gospel in the Lordship-salvation controversy. Ongoing dialogue between Roman Catholics and evangelicals has also raised questions about the meaning of the term *evangelical.* For example, Roman Catholic Keith A. Fournier describes himself as a "Catholic Evangelical." He explains that he embraces, not the Protestant doctrine of *sola fide,* but the gospel as defined by historic Roman Catholic thought.

In modern terminology the term *evangelical* tends to be defined either in terms of evangelistic methodology or by the notion that people need a personal conversion to Christ. If the term *evangelical* is used in the latter sense, then Charles Finney was certainly an evangelical. He clearly had a passion to see persons converted to Christ.

If we use the term *evangelical* in its classical sense, however, indicating one who embraces the doctrine of justification by faith alone, as formulated by the Reformers, then it would seem Finney was anything but an evangelical. Let us look briefly at his view regarding *sola fide.*

Justification: Not Forensic

Finney, having been trained in law, said that legally justification is a governmental action. It can be undertaken by the legislative or executive branch of government, but not by the judicial branch. A sinner can never be deemed "just" by the judicial branch. To do so would be to violate or deny the law itself.

"Gospel justification is the justification of sinners," Finney says. "It is, therefore, naturally impossible, and a most palpable contradiction, to affirm that the justification of a sinner, or of one who has violated the law, is a forensic or judicial justification. . . . Now it is certainly nonsense to affirm, that a sinner can be pronounced just in the eye of law; that he can be justified by deeds of law, or by the law at all. The law condemns him. But to be justified judicially or forensically, is to be pronounced just in the judgment of law. This certainly is an impossibility in respect to sinners."[8]

Finney is not merely quibbling over words here. He clearly understands that the forensic justification of which the Reformers spoke rests squarely on the imputation of Christ's righteousness to the believer. Only by being "in Christ" is the believer declared or reckoned just. Finney takes up the issue of such imputation later, so for now, we simply note in passing his awareness of it. It should also be pointed out that the Reformers believed, not that the sinner is justified by the law, but that the source of the forensic judgment is the Law-Giver, the Judge of all the earth and the executive arm of the universe.

Finney agrees that the sinner is governmentally treated as if he were just. But this rests not in the imputation of an "alien righteousness" as Martin Luther maintained, but simply in a decree of pardon or amnesty. He says that "sinners cannot possibly be just in any other sense."[9] He is sharply critical of the idea that justification is based on the imputation of Christ's righteousness to the believer. "The doctrine of an imputed righteousness, or that Christ's obedience to the law was accounted as our obedience," Finney wrote, "is founded on a most false and nonsensical assumption; to wit, that Christ owed no obedience to the law in His own person, and that therefore His obedience was altogether a work of supererogation, and might be made a substitute for our own obedience; that it might be set down to our credit, because He did not need to obey for Himself."[10]

Finney has erected a straw man of prodigious proportions. I know of no Reformer who taught that Christ did not need to obey the law in his own person. But Finney's point is that since Jesus was required in his humanity to be subject to the law at all points, his perfect obedience could earn no surplus merit that could then be given to others who lack such merit. Even Jesus was an "unprofitable servant" in this regard. Finney argues that it is impossible for any being to perform a work of supererogation. The only person Jesus could ever justify by his perfect obedience was himself.

This teaching in itself should be enough to demonstrate that Finney did not embrace the Protestant doctrine of *sola fide,* and his rejection of the imputation of Christ's righteousness to the believer greatly distances him from historical evangelicalism. But Finney did not reject imputation in a theological vacuum. It was inseparably linked to his doctrine of the atonement. In this regard, he has something in common with the Reformers, who also link justification with the atonement.

Classical evangelicalism rests justification on both the perfect active obedience of Christ and on his passive obedience on the cross. Two imputations occur: the sins of his people are imputed to Christ and borne by him on the cross; and Christ's righteousness is imputed to his people. Finney rejects both aspects of imputation, taking issue with the substitutionary and satisfaction view of Christ's atonement.

Atonement: Not Substitutionary

Perhaps there is no place in Finney's theology where it is more readily apparent that he departed from Christian orthodoxy than in his view of the atonement. Finney advocates what may be called the "governmental" or "moral influence" theory of the atonement, and it has more in common with the Socinian heresy than with evangelical orthodoxy.

Finney deems the satisfaction of God's retributive justice a manifest impossibility for anyone, even Christ, to accomplish: "It is naturally impossible, as it would require that satisfaction should be made to retributive justice. Strictly speaking, retributive justice can never be satisfied, in the sense that the guilty can be punished as much and as long as he deserves; for this would imply that he was punished until he ceased to be guilty, or became innocent. . . . To suppose, therefore, that Christ suffered in amount, all that was due to the elect, is to suppose that He suffered an eternal punishment multiplied by the whole number of the elect."[11]

It is beginning to become clear what B. B. Warfield had in mind when he said that if God were removed altogether from Finney's theology, there would be no essential change in its character. Perhaps Warfield sensed the repeated reference to law in the abstract, as if the law could be separated from the Law-Giver. The satisfaction view of the atonement does not see the law, in and of itself, as being satisfied, but rather the Father whose law it is that is satisfied. It is God who is both the Just and the Justifier. His justice is propitiated by Christ, and his demands are satisfied.

Finney did not deny the element of satisfaction altogether. He declared that "the atonement of Christ was intended as a satisfaction of public justice."[12] He seeks to explain this concept by appealing to natural theology. Several things can be learned from nature, which can teach that the human race is fallen, that God is benevolent, and that the quality of mercy is an attribute of God.

Finney expands this by saying: "It can also abundantly teach, that there is a real and a great danger in the exercise of mercy under a moral government, and supremely great under a government so vast and so enduring as the government of God; that, under such a government, the danger is very great, that the exercise of mercy will be understood as encouraging the hope of impunity in the commission of sin."[13]

One of Finney's chief concerns, which is expressed pervasively in his writings, is the threat of antinomianism. He seeks to guard the theology of the atonement from becoming an impetus to licentiousness. He lists several reasons for the necessity of the atonement, which include the following:

> ### Related Works by Finney
>
> *Systematic Theology.* 3d ed. 1878. Reprint. Edited by Dennis Carroll, Bill Nicely, and L. G. Parkhurst Jr. Minneapolis: Bethany, 1994.
>
> *The Memoirs of Charles G. Finney: The Complete Restored Text.* Edited by Garth M. Rosell and Richard A. G. Dupuis. Grand Rapids: Academie / Zondervan, 1989.

- An atonement was needed to promote the glory and influence of God in the universe. . . .
- An atonement was needed to present overpowering motives to repentance.
- An atonement was needed, that the offer of pardon might not seem like connivance at sin.
- An atonement was needed to manifest the sincerity of God in His legal enactments.
- An atonement was needed to make it safe to present the offer and promise of pardon.[14]

That the atonement of Christ was designed to satisfy the demand for public justice may be seen in Finney's further exposition of the matter:

Natural theology is abundantly competent to show, that God could not be just to His own intelligence, just to His character, and hence just to the universe, in dispensing with the execution of divine law, except upon the condition of providing a substitute of such a nature as to reveal as fully, and impress as deeply, the lessons that would be taught by the execution, as the execution itself would do. The great design of penalties is prevention, and this is of course the design of executing penalties. The head of every government is pledged to sustain the authority of law, by a due administration of rewards and punishments, and has no right in any instance to extend pardon, except upon conditions that will as effectually support the authority of law as the execution of its penalties would do. It was never found to be safe, or even possible under any government, to make the universal offer of pardon to violators of law, upon the bare condition of repentance, for the very obvious reason already suggested, that it would be a virtual repeal of all law. Public justice, by which every executive magistrate in the universe is bound, sternly and peremptorily forbids that mercy shall be extended to any culprit, without some equivalent being rendered to the government; that is, without something being done that will fully answer as a substitute for the execution of penalties.[15]

It is in this sense that Jesus "satisfies" public justice. His atonement guards against people's drawing a presumptive license from divine pardon or amnesty. The atonement spurs us on to acts of virtue and prevents or deters us from further sin. In this regard Christ serves as a model or exemplar for the wicked who may think that they can sin with impunity. Christ's sacrifice is not substitutionary for any individual's sin. It demonstrates God's commitment to law and moral virtue.

Finney saw the atonement as being designed for the benefit of the entire universe and everybody in it. It gives people "a higher knowledge of God than ever they had before, or ever could have gained in any other way."[16] This benefit is found chiefly in its revelatory character. It teaches that all mankind can be pardoned if they are rightly affected by it and brought to repentance.

We have seen that Finney's rejection of the Reformation doctrine of *sola fide* is linked to his view of the atonement. The "vicarious" atonement (vicarious in the sense explained above) is a condition of our justification. Other conditions include repentance and faith. With respect to faith, he remarks:

> I fear that there has been much of error in the conceptions of many upon this subject. They have talked of justification by faith, as if they supposed that, by an arbitrary appointment of God, faith was the condition, and the only condition of justification. This seems to be the antinomian view. The class of persons alluded to speak of justification by faith; as if it were by faith, and not by Christ through faith, that the penitent sinner is justified; as if faith, and not Christ, were our justification. They seem to regard faith not as a natural, but merely as a mystical condition of justification; as bringing us into a covenant and mystical relation to Christ, in consequence of which His righteousness or personal obedience is imputed to us. It should never be forgotten that the faith that is the condition of justification, is the faith that works by love.[17]

It is a bit difficult to sort out what Finney has in view here. In the first part of the paragraph, we wonder whose view of justification he is attacking. The Reformers would not assert that faith is an "arbitrary" appointment of God. Nor would they say that justification is by faith rather than by faith through Christ. What Finney attacks here would also be attacked by the Reformers, and both would agree that such a view is antinomian. But in the final part of the paragraph, Finney apparently does have the Reformation view in his sights. Again his rejection of the imputation of Christ's righteousness to the believer comes through loud and clear.

Sanctification: A Condition of Justification

Finney lists sanctification as another condition of (not the grounds for) justification. "Some theologians have made justification a condition of sanctification, instead of making sanctification a condition of justification," he says. "But this . . . is an erroneous view of the subject. . . . That present, full, and entire consecration of heart and life to God and His service, is an unalterable condition of present pardon of past sin, and of present acceptance with God."[18]

This last sentence is a fatal blow to the gospel of Jesus Christ. Gone is Luther's view of the justified sinner as being *simul iustus et peccator*. If full consecration of heart and life to God is an unalterable condition for pardon, who will be pardoned? This is not good news, but the worst of all possible news. If our justification rests on full sanctification, we of all people are most miserable. Finney makes abundantly clear what he is attacking:

> . . . Those who hold that justification by imputed righteousness is a forensic proceeding, take a view of final or ultimate justification, according with their view of the nature of the transaction. With them, faith receives an imputed righteousness, and a judicial justification. The first act of faith, according to them, introduces the sinner into this relation, and obtains for him a perpetual justification. They maintain that after this first act of faith it is impossible for the sinner to come into condemnation; that, being once justified, he is always thereafter justified, whatever he may do; indeed that he is never justified by grace, as to sins that are past, upon condition that he ceases to sin; that Christ's righteousness is the ground, and that his own present obedience is not even a condition of his justification, so that, in fact, his own present or future obedience to the law of God is, in no case, and in no sense, a *sine qua non* of his justification, present or ultimate.

Now this is certainly another gospel from the one I am inculcating. It is not a difference merely upon some speculative or theoretic point. It is a point fundamental to the gospel and to salvation, if any one can be.[19]

Just when I think Finney grasps the Reformation view of *sola fide,* he surprises me by articulating a confused view of it. He says the view he rejects teaches that once the sinner is justified he is "always thereafter justified, whatever he may do." In one sense this is true of the Reformed view, but it is dangerously misleading. "Whatever he may do" may imply that the justified sinner may continue merrily in sin without any fruit of sanctification and still be justified. The Reformers stressed that, though justification is by faith alone, the faith that is the instrumental cause of justification is not a faith that is alone. True, saving faith yields necessarily the fruit of sanctification, though this fruit is not the ground of justification.

A technical point must be mentioned here. When Finney says that "in no case, and in no sense, [is obedience] a *sine qua non* of his justification," we might be inclined to agree. The technical point is this: The Reformed view does, in a narrow sense, see obedience as a "condition" (but never the ground) of justification. It is a condition, not in the sense that it must be met before the sinner can be declared just, but in the sense that it is a necessary fruit of genuine faith. The real necessary condition is the presence of real faith, which will of necessity yield the fruit of obedience. If no obedience follows, then no true faith was ever present.

Related Works about Finney

Hardman, Keith J. *Charles Grandison Finney, 1792–1875: Revivalist and Reformer.* 1987. Reprint. Grand Rapids: Baker, 1990.

Charles Grandison Finney: 19th Century Giant of American Revivalism (1792–1875). Christian History, 7, 4 (1988). The entire issue (no. 20) is devoted to Finney.

Warfield, Benjamin Breckinridge. "The Theology of Charles G. Finney." In Benjamin Breckinridge Warfield. *Perfectionism.* Edited by Ethelbert D. Warfield et al. 2 vols. 1931–32. Reprint. Grand Rapids: Baker, 1981. 2:166–215. Also in Benjamin Breckinridge Warfield. *Perfectionism.* Edited by Samuel G. Craig. Philadelphia: Presbyterian and Reformed, 1958. Pages 166–215.

Finney rightly asserts that a faith without works or obedience is antinomian. But the Reformers taught justification, not by the profession of faith alone, but by the possession of faith (a *fides viva*) alone.

Finney then warms to the task of attacking *sola fide*.

> If the view of justification I am opposing be true, it is altogether out of place for one who has once believed, to ask for the pardon of sin. It is a downright insult to God, and apostasy from Christ. . . .
>
> If I understand the framers of *The Westminster Confession of Faith,* they regarded justification as a state resulting from the relation of an adopted child of God, which state is entered into by faith alone, and held that justification is not conditionated upon obedience for the time being, but that a person in this state may, as they hold that all in this life in fact do, sin daily, and even continually, yet without condemnation by the law, their sin bringing them only under his fatherly displeasure, and subjecting them to the necessity of repentance, as a condition of his fatherly favor, but not as a condition of pardon or of ultimate salvation. They seem to have regarded the child of God as no longer under moral government, in such a sense that sin was imputed to him, this having been imputed to Christ, and Christ's righteousness so literally imputed to him that, do what he may, after the first act of faith he is accounted and treated in his person as wholly righteous. If this is not antinomianism, I know not what is; since they hold that all who once believe will certainly be saved, yet that their perseverance in holy obedience to the end is, in no case, a condition of final justification, but that this is conditionated upon the first act of faith alone. . . .[20]

I am not totally willing to grant the "if" of Finney's understanding of *The Westminster Confession of Faith.* He seems determined to read into it an antinomian spin. But he gets enough of the main drift of *The Confession* to reject its basic position on justification.

I have labored Finney's view of justification for two reasons: to show that in fact he was not an "evangelical" in the historic sense, and to prepare us to see that behind his own view of justification and the atonement is a fundamentally Pelagian view of man and his will. Finney concludes his treatment of justification by saying:

> The relations of the old school view of justification to their view of depravity is obvious. They hold . . . that the constitution in every faculty and part is sinful. Of course, a return to personal, present holiness, in the sense of entire conformity to the law, cannot with them be a condition of justification. They must have a justification while yet at least in some degree of sin. This must be brought about by imputed righteousness. The intellect revolts at a justification in sin. So a scheme is devised to divert the eye of the law and of the lawgiver from the sinner to his substitute, who has perfectly obeyed the law. . . . Constitutional depravity or sinfulness being once assumed, physical regeneration, physical sanctification, physical divine influence, imputed righteousness and justification, while personally in the commission of sin, follow of course.[21]

Moral Depravity: Not a Sinful Nature

Finney develops his view of sin in his discussion of moral depravity. He begins by making an important distinction between moral and physical depravity. His use of the word *physical* may seem strange to modern ears, because he is not referring exclusively to that which is bodily or corporeal. He seems to use the term in a manner suggestive of its derivation from *physis* ("nature"). He says:

> Physical depravity, as the word denotes, is the depravity of constitution, or substance, as distinguished from depravity of free moral action. It may be predicated of body or of mind. Physical depravity, when predicated of the body, is commonly and rightly called disease. . . . When physical depravity is predicated of mind, it is intended that the powers of the mind, either in substance, or in consequence of their connection with, and dependence upon, the body, are in a diseased, lapsed, fallen, degenerate state, so that the healthy action of those powers is not sustained.

Physical depravity, being depravity of substance as opposed to depravity of the actions of free will, can have no moral character. . . . physical depravity, whether of body or of mind, can have no moral character in itself, for the plain reason that it is involuntary, and in its nature is disease, and not sin. Let this be remembered.[22]

That Finney exhorts the reader to remember his statements regarding physical depravity indicates the importance he attaches to them.

Finney then defines moral depravity so that it can only be predicated of violations of moral law. Moral depravity is sin and "sin must consist in choice."[23] Moral depravity is not a sinful nature but a sinful heart. Finney acknowledges that all mankind are both physically and morally depraved. Man has a physically depraved nature, but this is not a sinful nature. "Moral depravity," he concludes, "is not then to be accounted for by ascribing it to a nature or constitution sinful in itself."[24] He says: "But writers on moral depravity have assumed, that moral depravity was distinct from, and the cause of sin, that is, of actual transgression. They call it original sin, indwelling sin, a sinful nature, an appetite for sin, an attribute of human nature, and the like."[25]

Finney was probably aware of the classic distinction between *original sin* and *actual sin.* This distinction describes the difference between the activity of sinning and the morally depraved nature that produces sinful activity. This distinction functions in a way similar to the one Jesus made between corrupt fruit and the corrupt tree that yields this fruit.

Finney struggled against this for many reasons, perhaps chiefly to avoid the conclusion that man cannot not sin *(non posse non peccare)* and whose sin would thereby be excusable. He records several objections to original sin: "I object to the doctrine of constitutional sinfulness, that it makes all sin original and actual, a mere calamity, and not a crime. . . . If the nature is sinful, in such a sense that action must necessarily be sinful, which is the doctrine of the Confession of Faith, then sin in action must be a calamity, and can be no crime. It is the necessary effect of a sinful nature. This cannot be a crime, since the will has nothing to do with it."[26]

We may disregard for the moment that according to the confession of faith to which Finney refers the will has everything to do with it. Finney grants that Adam's sin had a negative influence on subsequent generations, but he denies that one such influence was an inherited sinful nature. "The dogma of constitutional moral depravity," he says, "is a part and parcel of the doctrine of a necessitated will. It is a branch of a grossly false and heathenish philosophy. How infinitely absurd, dangerous, and unjust, then, to embody it in a standard of Christian doctrine, to give it the place of an indispensable article of faith, and denounce all who will not swallow its absurdities, as heretics!"[27]

At the heart of Finney's theology is the conviction that man has a free will: Man has not only the natural ability to make choices, but also the moral ability to make proper choices. He categorically rejects Jonathan Edwards's view of moral inability, and by implication Augustine's distinction between free will and liberty. "The human will is free," he says, "therefore men have power or ability to do all their duty. The moral government of God everywhere assumes and implies the liberty of the human will, and the natural ability of men to obey God. Every command, every threatening, every expostulation and denunciation in the Bible implies and assumes this."[28]

Finney fiercely opposes the distinction made by Edwards in *The Freedom of the Will* between natural and moral ability, seeing it as a distinction without a difference. "Let the impression, then, be distinct," he says, "that the Edwardean natural ability is no ability at all, and nothing but an empty name, a metaphysico-theological fiction."[29] Finney does not like Edwards's insistence that all choices are determined by prior inclinations or motives. Finney sees this as a rejection of the sovereign power of the agent, resulting in choices being governed, not by the will, but by motive. If the will is bound by a motive and lacks the power in itself to determine its own motives freely, according to Finney, then man has neither natural nor moral ability.

When Edwards spoke of natural ability, he restricted it to the ability to choose what one is motivated or inclined to choose.

Man's moral inability resides in his being a slave to his own corrupt motives or inclinations, a corruption that is part of his constitutive nature. This corruption results from and is linked to original sin.

Finney's categorical rejection of original sin leads him to reject any notion of bondage to sin. Finney argues that if man is morally unable to obey God, then he has neither freedom nor obligation. "Natural ability and natural liberty to will, must then be identical," he says. "Let this be distinctly remembered, since many have scouted the doctrine of natural ability to obey God, who have nevertheless been great sticklers for the freedom of the will. In this they are greatly inconsistent. This ability is called a natural ability, because it belongs to man as a moral agent, in such a sense that without it he could not be a proper subject of command, of reward or punishment. That is, without this liberty or ability he could not be a moral agent, and a proper subject of moral government."[30]

Finney's argument follows closely that of Pelagius. Both reason from the premise of duty and obligation to moral ability. Their controlling assumption is that if God requires something from the creature, the creature must have the ability to meet the requirement. Moral obligation demands moral ability.

Finney objected that Edwards denied that moral agents are not the cause of their own actions, and affirmed that such actions are caused by motives. But Finney's objection misses Edwards's point altogether. Edwards did not abstract motive from the agent who has these motives. By acting according to motive, the agent is still doing the willing and still acting with self-determination. Edwards affirmed that the self is determining the choice and is enslaved to sinful motives.

Regeneration: Dependent on Our Decision

When Finney moves to the subject of regeneration, we see his synergism with utmost clarity. Finney distinguishes between regeneration and conversion: "Conversion, as it implies and expresses the activity and turning of the subject, does not include and imply any Divine agency, and therefore does not imply or express what is intended by regeneration. As two agencies are actually employed in the regeneration and conversion of a sinner, it is necessary to adopt terms that will clearly teach this fact, and clearly distinguish between the agency of God and of the creature."[31]

According to Finney regeneration consists in a change in the attitude of the will or in its ultimate choice, intention, or preference. In this change the creature is both passive and active. Finney explains it by saying:

> . . . he is passive in the perception of the truth presented by the Holy Spirit. I know that this perception is no part of regeneration. But it is simultaneous with regeneration. It induces regeneration. It is the condition and the occasion of regeneration. Therefore the subject of regeneration must be a passive recipient or percipient of the truth presented by the Holy Spirit, at the moment, and during the act of regeneration. The Spirit acts upon him through or by the truth: thus far he is passive. He closes with the truth: thus far he is active. . . . Neither God, nor any other being, can regenerate him, if he will not turn. If he will not change his choice, it is impossible that it should be changed. . . .
> . . . It is a change of choice, or of intention. . . .[32]

Finney rejects the idea that regeneration involves a change in the sinner's constituent nature effected by the Holy Spirit alone. Rather "regeneration consists in the sinner changing his ultimate choice, intention, [or] preference."[33]

For Finney, regeneration rests and depends on the decision or choice of the sinner. Regeneration follows from a human decision. At this point Finney's theology has had a massive influence on modern evangelism, which makes a "decision" the necessary prerequisite for regeneration. Modern evangelists frequently call sinners to choose to be born again or to make a decision to be regenerated. Here faith precedes regeneration and is a necessary condition for regeneration and/or conversion. It is precisely at this point that the doctrine of *sola gratia* is severely compromised. It is at this point that Pelagianism has a stranglehold on the evangelical church today.

Though divine persuasion
be limitless,
it still remains persuasion,
and so when a decision
is secured for Christ
in the individual
he exercises his own will
apart from even a shadow
of constraint.

Lewis Sperry Chafer

We Are Able to Believe:
Lewis Sperry Chafer

ispensationalism has become widely popular within evangelical Christianity. This system of doctrine is probably the dominant theology in American evangelicalism today, and it has a massive influence internationally as well. Many people view Dispensationalism as merely a specific approach to eschatology. Historically, however, Dispensationalism has a full-orbed theological system that has much to say about soteriology.

Currently Dispensationalism appears to be going through certain changes in emphasis and even in doctrine. In light of the Lordship-salvation controversy that originated within Dispensational circles but generated controversy within the broader evangelical world as well, Dispensationalists have set about the task of clarifying doctrinal positions on related matters. The developments within Dispensational thought, particularly those evidenced at Dallas Theological Seminary, are encouraging to advocates of classical Reformed theology.

Because Dispensationalism is in a state of flux, it is dangerous and misleading to regard Dispensational theology as monolithic, particularly with respect to soteriology. In this chapter we will focus chiefly on the system of theology worked out by Lewis Sperry Chafer, who has exercised enormous influence on Dispensational thought.

A critical point of interest for us will be the relationship of Dispensationalism to historical Calvinism and Augustinianism. Is Dispensationalism at its core Augustinian or semi-Pelagian? Surely many, if not most Dispensationalists would answer this question by clearly affirming Augustinianism and eschewing semi-Pelagianism. Dispensationalists frequently claim they are "four-point Calvinists," affirming total depravity, unconditional election, irresistible grace, and perseverance of the saints, but rejecting limited atonement.

In his book *Wrongly Dividing the Word of Truth*, Reformed scholar John H. Gerstner concluded that Dispensationalism is "spurious Calvinism."[1] Many in the Dispensational community protested, pleading that Gerstner had misunderstood historic Dispensationalism. This plea was coupled with a strong reaffirmation that Dispensationalism is indeed four-point Calvinism.

In my discussions with Dispensational thinkers, I have probed their four-point Calvinism, having had difficulty understanding how a person can hold to the four points they espouse and yet reject the fifth. In some of these discussions, I discovered what appeared to be a misunderstanding of the four points and a clear understanding of the fifth. I came away thinking that they did not embrace the four points as historically understood by Calvinism. In some of these conversations, on the other hand, I heard a clear affirmation of the four points and a misunderstanding of limited atonement. Still a third group seemed to embrace the four points in their historical sense while rejecting limited atonement in its historical sense. The universe of my experience provides an inadequate basis from which to draw final conclusions about Dispensationalism today, but it does point out that no small amount of confusion exists regarding these issues.

Total Depravity?

1871	Born in Rock Creek, Ohio
1877	Converted to Christ
1888	Enrolled in Oberlin College
1896	Married Ella Loraine Case
1900	Ordained in Buffalo, New York
1902	Became active in Northfield Conference
1911	Joined staff of Scofield School of the Bible
1924	Became president and professor of Evangelical Theological College (later Dallas Theological Seminary)
1947–48	Published *Systematic Theology*
1952	Died in Seattle, Wash.

As we turn our attention to the theology of Lewis Sperry Chafer, we will look first at his view of original sin, which bears heavily on the first of the five points, total depravity. Chafer says original sin involves what he calls the *sin nature*. "In seeking to analyze more specifically what the sin nature is," he writes, "it should be remembered that it is a perversion of God's original creation and in that sense is an abnormal thing. Every faculty of man is injured by the fall and the disability to do good, and the strange predisposition to evil arises from that inner confusion."[2]

Chafer speaks of the disability to do good, which corresponds to the Augustinian notion of moral inability. That man is born in a state of corruption and that actual sin flows from this corrupt nature is central to Chafer's view. "As every effect must have its cause, there is a cause or reason for the fact that personal sin is universal," he says. "That cause is the sin nature—sometimes styled the *Adamic nature, inborn sin, original sin*, or the *old man*. By whatever term it is indicated, the reference is to a reality which originated with Adam and has been transmitted from Adam to all his race. The effect of the first sin upon unfallen Adam was a degeneration—a conversion downwards."[3]

Here Chafer identifies original sin as a condition transmitted from Adam to his posterity. At this point Chafer is in complete agreement with Augustine and in sharp disagreement with Pelagius. "As an immediate result of that first sin," Chafer declares, "Adam became a different kind of being from that which God had created, and the law of generation obtained, which sees to it that reproduction by any living thing will be 'after its kind.'"[4] To say that Adam became a "different kind of being" does not mean that Adam ceased to be *human*. Rather Chafer is speaking of the moral difference between Adam's being before the fall and his being after the fall.

In his exposition of man's sin nature, Chafer quotes W. G. T. Shedd at length and with approval, then comments: "Following this exhaustive statement regarding the condition of the understanding and will as influenced by the fallen nature, Dr. Shedd writes with equal force on the question of the fallen nature and its guilt. This issue which has so divided the two major schools—Calvinists and Arminians—is not only clearly stated by Dr. Shedd in defense of the Calvinistic view, but that which he has written serves to expose the shallow rationalism which the Arminian notion presents."[5]

Chafer seeks to distance himself from the Arminian view of depravity and to side with historic Calvinism. He argues that men are born spiritually dead, leaving them incapable of doing any spiritual good with respect to salvation.

We have seen that the historic controversy over free will is inseparably related to the doctrine of original sin. With that in mind, we now look to Chafer's view of free will. He treats this subject in conjunction with the divine decrees. "If God be sovereign and only those things occur which are determined in His decree," Chafer asks, "is there any sphere left in which a creature may exercise his own free will?"[6]

He answers: "The human choice of that which is good, like the choice of that which is evil, originates *within,* as the individual's volition and is *free* in the sense that the individual is not conscious of any necessity being imposed upon him. All human action is included in this conception. Since human action appears to be restrained by nothing other than moral suasion or by emotions, the interrogation is in order as to what extent the human will is free."[7]

For Chafer, free will refers to man's ability to act according to his own desires, a view that follows the Augustinian notion. This freedom operates within the broader scope of divine sovereignty. Man's free will is an instrument through which God brings about his sovereign plan. "When exercising his will, man is conscious only of his freedom of action," Chafer says. "He determines his course by circumstances, but God is the author of circumstances. Man is impelled by emotions, but God is able to originate and to control every human emotion. . . . God will mold and direct in all secondary causes until His own eternal purpose is realized."[8]

Chafer does not analyze in depth the nature of human freedom. He is content to let John Dick speak for him: ". . . liberty consist[s] in the power of acting according to the prevailing inclination, or the motive which appears strongest to the mind. Those actions are free which are the effect of volition. In whatever manner the state of mind which gave rise to the volition has been produced, the liberty of the agent is neither greater nor less. . . . Liberty does not consist in the power of acting or not acting, but in acting from choice. The choice is determined by something in the mind itself, or by something external influencing the mind; but, whatever is the cause, the choice makes the action free, and the agent accountable."[9]

There is a degree of vagueness in both Chafer's view of freedom and Dick's. On the surface both seem to adopt Edwards's view. But Chafer's treatment of the question is brief and fails to analyze closely the work of the will. We must withhold judgment until we see how Chafer understands the work of the will in regeneration.

Conditional Regeneration

When we turn to Chafer's (and historic Dispensationalism's) view of regeneration, we focus on what I believe is the most crucial point of the debate between Dispensationalism and Reformed theology. Here the question of Dispensationalism's four-point Calvinism becomes acute.

Remember that in Reformed theology's *ordo salutis,* regeneration precedes faith. It does so with respect to *logical priority,* not *temporal priority.* Reformed theology grants that God's act of regeneration and the believer's act of faith are simultaneous, not separated, with respect to time. The *ordo salutis* refers to logical dependency. Faith logically depends on regeneration; regeneration does not logically depend on faith. Again, the *priority* is logical, not temporal. Regeneration is the necessary condition of faith; faith is not the necessary condition of or for regeneration.

The logical priority of regeneration in Reformed theology rests on the doctrine of total depravity or moral inability. Because fallen man is morally unable to incline himself by faith to Christ, regeneration is a logical necessity for faith to occur. If we were to posit that faith precedes regeneration, then we would be assuming that unregenerate people, while still in an unregenerate state, have the moral ability to exercise faith. If the unregenerate can exercise faith, then it follows clearly that they are not fallen to the degree of moral inability, as claimed by classical Augustinian and Reformed theology. This would involve an Arminian or semi-Pelagian view of the fall.

It is also important to note that Reformed theology understands regeneration to involve a change in the fallen human being's nature. That is, the human nature itself undergoes a change in its constitution. The question we face, then, is this: Are Chafer and Dispensationalism, as they claim to be, Calvinistic?

In his *Systematic Theology* Chafer declares: "This means that God's answer to an individual's faith in Christ is such that by the power of God he is born of God and thus becomes an actual son of His."[10] This statement makes it clear that rebirth (the subject Chafer is discussing here) is wrought by God *in response* to man's faith. Faith occurs before God "answers."

Perhaps this statement represents a mere "slip of the pen" and other statements can be found to offset this one. One more statement by Chafer, however, removes all doubt about the order of faith and regeneration in his system: "On the human side, regeneration is conditioned simply on faith."[11]

In light of this statement, we can justly call Chafer's position "conditional regeneration." This does not mean that once a person is regenerated he must meet certain conditions to remain regenerated. That is, it does not refer to *temporary* or *provisional* regeneration. The condition of which Chafer writes refers to that which must first be met before regeneration occurs. This condition is *faith*. If regeneration is conditioned on faith, then in terms of logical priority it certainly must not *precede* faith.

The historic controversy between Augustinianism and semi-Pelagianism has often been described as a conflict over *monergism* and *synergism*. Semi-Pelagianism sees human cooperation as a necessary ingredient in regeneration. At this point Chafer

Related Works by Chafer
Grace. 1922. Reprint. Grand Rapids: Kregel, 1995.
Salvation. 1917. Reprint. Grand Rapids: Kregel, 1991.
Systematic Theology. 8 vols. 1947–48. Reprint. Grand Rapids: Kregel, 1993.

emphatically rejects synergism and affirms monergism. He quotes John F. Walvoord approvingly:

> Pelagian and Arminian theologians, holding as they do to the cooperation of the human will and the partial ability of the will through common grace or natural powers, recognize to some extent the presence of means in the work of regeneration. If the total inability of man be recognized, and the doctrine of efficacious grace believed, it naturally follows that regeneration is accomplished apart from means. Reformed theology in keeping with its doctrine of efficacious grace has held that the human will in itself is ineffectual in bringing about any of the changes incident to salvation of the soul. As related to faith, the human will can act by means of efficacious grace. The human will can act even apart from efficacious grace in hearing the Gospel. In the act of regeneration, however, the human will is entirely passive. There is no cooperation possible. The nature of the work of regeneration forbids any possible human assistance. . . . In the new birth, of course, the human will is not opposed to regeneration and wills by divine grace to believe, but this act in itself does not produce new birth. . . . in the work of regeneration, the human will is entirely passive. . . . It is rather that regeneration is wholly a work of God in a believing heart.[12]

With utmost clarity this passage affirms the monergistic character of regeneration. While eschewing Arminianism and Pelagianism, Chafer and Walvoord affirm both the total inability of man and the efficacious grace of God. Man is passive in regeneration, which is *solely* the work of God.

Does not this mean that these men clearly side with Reformed theology and affirm monergism? Though it may appear so at first glance, sadly it is not the case at all. What we see here is some-thing of the traditional "red herring." The classic dispute over monergism and synergism is not over the question of who does the regenerating. Virtually everyone agrees that only God can do the work of regeneration proper.

The issue focuses instead on what the unregenerate person can do to evoke the divine work of regeneration. Synergists hold that one can "choose Christ" or "believe in Christ" prior to regen-eration. The choice or the act of faith is a condition for regener-ation. It is at this point that they are synergistic. The grace of regeneration is offered, but the "efficacious" grace of regenera-tion is given only to those who first accept the offer or act in faith to receive it.

Walvoord says that "regeneration is wholly a work of God in a believing heart." This statement is a bit unclear. It clearly intends to affirm that regeneration is wholly the work of God and in no degree the work of man. But what does Walvoord mean by the phrase "in a believing heart?" Is the heart already believing, or is it believing because it has been regenerated? The answer to this question defines the difference between Calvinism and semi-Pelagianism. In normal language the Calvinist would say that regeneration is the work of God in the unbelieving heart by which the unbelieving heart is changed into a believing heart.

In similar fashion Chafer elsewhere declares: ". . . the believer is regenerated and thus is introduced into a new estate, a new existence, a new relationship which is well defined as a new cre-ation."[13] The grammar of this statement indicates that this regen-eration and introduction are accorded to believers, not to unbe-lievers. The language is vague, which vagueness would be removed entirely if Chafer would have said simply that "the unbe-liever is regenerated . . ."

In his critique of Dispensationalism, John Gerstner wrote:

> All of these theologians preach salvation by grace and they seem to recognize this state of sin from which no one can be rescued except through the atoning blood of Jesus Christ. . . .
> In spite of this, the dispensational view of the totally depraved man is one who is not totally depraved after all. It turns out that

he is not totally disabled. According to the Reformed doctrine, total depravity makes man *morally* incapable of making a virtuous choice. While Dispensationalism seems to go along with this idea to a degree, this "totally depraved" man is nevertheless able to believe. We shall see that his faith precedes or is at least simultaneous with (and not based upon) his regeneration. As long as that doctrine is maintained, the nerve of total depravity is cut. If total depravity does anything, it renders man totally unable because he is indisposed to respond to the overtures of grace. If the dispensationalist maintains, as he does, that man is *morally* able to respond to the gospel, then Dispensationalism does not believe that man is totally depraved after all.[14]

Impartation of the Divine Nature

When Chafer explains regeneration, we see that there is a marked difference between his understanding of it and that of Reformed theology. For Chafer regeneration involves God's impartation of the divine nature to the believer:

> ... the impartation of the very life of God is one of the most important features of the whole transforming undertaking. The receiving of the divine nature means that the individual thus blessed has been born of God. ... This is a change so radical and so complete that there is thus achieved a passing from one order of being into another. Eventually in this great change the Adamic nature will be dismissed and the ego as a separate entity will represent little else than the stupendous fact of being a son of God and a rightful member in the family and household of God. ... The conception that regeneration by the Holy Spirit is an indefinite influence for good in the individual's present life is far below the conception set forth in the New Testament. There it is taught that a new and eternal order of being is created with indissoluble filial relations to the Creator of all things.[15]

Chafer later repeats the same assertion: "Closely allied to the gift of eternal life is the impartation of the divine nature. ... No comparison may be drawn between the acquiring of a human nature and the acquiring of the divine nature."[16]

Again Chafer supports his view by appealing to the words of Walvoord: "The figure of creation indicates that regeneration is creative in its nature and results in a fundamental change in the individual, a new nature being added with its new capacities."[17]

Of course Reformed theology agrees that regeneration is creative and that it results in a fundamental change in the individual. It involves a new nature. But this new nature is a new *human* nature; it is not a divine nature. Reformed theology also affirms that with regeneration comes also the added benefit of the indwelling of the Holy Spirit. But this indwelling is not the act of regeneration itself.

The idea that regeneration involves a kind of apotheosis is not without precedent in church history. It can be found, for example, in the thought of Athanasius and other church fathers. In our time it is taught by men such as Paul Crouch, who has repeatedly asserted that the believing, regenerate Christian is as much the incarnation of God as Jesus was.[18]

In his critique Gerstner provides a table that succinctly displays the differences between historic Calvinism and Dispensationalism at key points. Under the rubric of the perseverance of the saints, he summarizes Dispensationalism: "The 'regenerate' new nature, being divine, can never sin or perish, while the old nature is unaffected by it and continues to operate sinfully, as before regeneration, until destroyed at death."[19]

This view of regeneration likely accounts for the possibility commonly held by modern Dispensationalists of the so-called "carnal" Christian. This is a person who has received Jesus as Savior but has not yet submitted to him as Lord. This person is still basically carnal in orientation, but he enjoys his "position" of being justified. He is not yet filled with the Spirit.

This view has been popularized by Campus Crusade's famous booklet *The Four Spiritual Laws*. In an illustration three circles are displayed, and an outline of a chair occupies the center of each circle. In the first circle, the self is enthroned on the chair. The symbol for Christ is placed outside the circle. This circle represents the unregenerate unbeliever. In the second circle the self is again seated on the throne, but the symbol for Christ now appears inside the circle. This circle represents the carnal Christian, who is in a state of grace and is "saved," but who has not yet cooperated with the indwelling Spirit. In the third circle, depicting the Spirit-filled life, Christ is seated on the throne.

This illustration may indicate several things. First, regeneration does not necessarily effect a change in the believer's constituent nature. The believer may be regenerated, but his life is still dominated by the self or the old, Adamic nature. The Spirit of God dwells within him. He has this new divine nature, but he has not yet cooperated with it to effect a change in his life. Only when the old man cooperates with the indwelling Spirit does the Spirit-filled life occur. Second, righteousness performed by the Christian is performed not by his human nature per se, but by the Holy Spirit.

Related Works about Chafer

Blaising, Craig A. "Lewis Sperry Chafer." In Walter A. Elwell, ed. *Handbook of Evangelical Theologians.* Grand Rapids: Baker, 1993. Pages 83–96.

Gerstner, John H. *Wrongly Dividing the Word of Truth.* Brentwood, Tenn.: Wolgemuth & Hyatt, 1991.

Hannah, John D. "The Early Years of Lewis Sperry Chafer." *Bibliotheca Sacra* 144 (Jan. 1987): 3–23.

In analyzing the thought of J. F. Strombeck on this point, Gerstner observes: "There are, in the converted person, presumably two natures—an old nature which is altogether evil and which produces only wood, hay, and stubble; and a new nature which, being altogether divine, of course produces nothing but gold, silver, and precious stones. In other words, the genuinely human nature produces nothing but useless works which will be consumed by fire. God, dwelling in the 'saint,' produces nothing but absolutely excellent, divinely approved works. This . . . shows clearly that what they are thinking of is the works of man versus the works of God and not works of the sinful man contrasted with the works of the converted man."[20]

Irresistible Grace?

We see that since Chafer makes regeneration dependent on faith, his view is inconsistent with the Reformed concept of total depravity. Was he then a "three-point" Calvinist? Let us look next at his view of irresistible grace.

Chafer commits himself to the "efficacious call" of God. Obviously he intends to echo the Reformed doctrine of effectual calling, which is in view in the doctrine of irresistible grace. He writes:

> An efficacious call to salvation, then, is a call which none ever finally resists (cf. Rom. 8:30). Everyone whom God predestinates He calls, and everyone whom he calls He justifies and glorifies. . . . The vision which He creates in the heart and the limitless persuasion He exercises induce a favorable reaction on the part of all thus called, which reaction is rendered infinitely certain. The important truth to be observed in all of this is that, though divine persuasion be limitless, it still remains persuasion, and so when a decision is secured for Christ in the individual he exercises his own will apart from even a shadow of constraint. The divine invitation still is true that "whosoever will may come." However, it also is true that none will ever come apart from this divine call, and that the call is extended only to His elect.[21]

Chafer appears to be saying that the call God gives only to the elect is efficacious, but not inherently irresistible. It is always effective because the persuasion is so strong. But its efficacy still rests on the unconstrained human will, and this without the benefit of regeneration. God's call is a *sine qua non* for salvation, but so is the sinner's response.

Reformed theology agrees that our response to the inner call of God is a free one, in that the subject exercises his choice freely. But Reformed theology also affirms that the work of regeneration so changes the disposition of the soul that the soul is truly made willing, and this is foreign to Chafer's view. So Chafer is not in harmony with the I of TULIP, irresistible grace.

In his critique of Dispensational views of irresistible grace, John Gerstner points to the most famous Dispensationalist of them all, Billy Graham. Gerstner cites Graham's book *How To Be Born Again:*

> Graham writes that the "new birth is something that God does for man *when man is willing to yield* to God." Again, "Any person who

is willing to trust Jesus Christ as his personal Savior and Lord can receive the new birth now." Significantly, he also says that a "person cannot turn to God to repent or even to believe without God's help. God must do the turning." One can see from this that Graham is Arminian and not Pelagian. This could also be said of most dispensationalists. That is, divine "help" is needed, but not divine regeneration. A man cannot believe without help, but he cannot be regenerated without believing. This is precisely the evangelical Arminian order—divine help, then human faith, followed by regeneration.[22]

Gerstner continues his analysis of Graham:

Graham goes on to make his Arminian thinking quite clear. Whatever the necessary "help" is, it is not regeneration. "The Holy Spirit will do everything possible to disturb you, draw you, love you— but finally it is your personal decision. . . . Make it happen now." Billy Graham is not a professional theologian, but the professional theologians whom he follows are just as explicit. "It is entirely a supernatural act of God *in response to the faith of man,*" say Chafer and Walvoord.[23]

Unconditional Election?

Much of the debate over free will is tied to the doctrine of election. Since Chafer claims to hold the Reformed view of predestination, we must now examine that claim.

Chafer seems to take a strong stand in favor of unconditional election: ". . . the divine decree is absolutely *unconditional,*" he says. "The execution of it is in no way suspended upon conditions which may or may not emerge. The Arminian notion that the will of man is sovereign in its power to resist the Almighty must be denied, since it is everywhere refuted in the history of God's dealing with men. God may, for good reasons, allow man's will to prevail, but He does not have to do so. He has power over every will to cause it to do His good pleasure."[24]

Chafer clearly wants to distance himself from Arminianism, and he does deny the Arminian notion that the human will has the sovereign power to resist the divine decree. We have already seen that Chafer's irresistible grace is the grace of persuasion, a persuasion so convincing that no one will ever reject it. Nevertheless, it is important to recall that Chafer regards faith as a condition for regeneration. That condition is met as a result of the divine persuasion, which leads to faith and in turn to regeneration.

That God sovereignly guarantees that the condition of faith is met by the elect indicates Chafer's agreement with Reformed theology at this point. How Chafer says that condition is met, however, differs sharply from Reformed theology. In Reformed theology the condition of faith is met in the elect as a result of regeneration. This involves more than divine persuasion, but not less.

Chafer also seeks to distance himself from the prescient view of election, according to which God elects on the basis of foreseen faith. "This notion is advanced by those who maintain that God's decrees are conditional, to the end that some are chosen to eternal life on the basis of divine foresight as to their faith and obedience," Chafer says. "This theory, if it were true, would support the wholly unscriptural idea that, in the end, men are saved on the ground of their own merit and worthiness. This claim not only opposes the doctrine of salvation by grace alone, but leaves the question as to whether God is the Author of sin unanswered and places God in the unworthy position of being dependent upon His creatures."[25]

Later Chafer concludes: "Published systems of theology which either omit the doctrine of divine decree, or oppose the doctrine, are justly reprehensible."[26]

Other Dispensationalists

John Gerstner laments that the Dispensational sound on unconditional election is uncertain at best. He cites other writers to indicate that many Dispensationalists diverge from this doctrine. He points to the note on 1 Peter 1:2 in the *Scofield Reference Bible*, which declares, "election is according to the foreknowledge of God, and wholly of grace, apart from human merit."[27]

"So we see what is meant by unconditional election," Gerstner observes. "It is unconditional *justification* that dispensationalists are talking about. One can see by this statement that the *Scofield* editors view God as foreseeing that the sinner will repent. Because God foresees this repentance and belief of the sinner, He, without any meritorious condition on the sinner's part, chooses him to everlasting life. That is to say, He elects the sinner without the sinner having *any condition of virtue* which recommends him for election."[28]

Gerstner, who reminds us that this is not the Reformed view of unconditional election, points to similar ideas in the writings of Harry A. Ironside, Charles C. Ryrie, and Norman L. Geisler. He says of the latter:

> In Norman Geisler, the implicit Arminianism of Dispensationalism has become explicit. This former Dallas Seminary professor . . . very clearly makes the divine purposes in salvation entirely dependent upon human choice. Geisler writes, "God would save all men if He could. . . . God will achieve the greatest number in heaven [that] He possibly can." The limitation on the divine will is human will. God will save as many as God can "without violating their free choice." Divine election is clearly dependent on the human sinner's "free choice." No Arminian has ever been more specific in his denial of Calvinistic doctrine than this self-designated dispensational Calvinist. Geisler not only denies the fourth point, "irresistible grace," but unconditional election as well because, emphatically, he makes divine election the result of fallen man's "free will." [29]

What exactly does Geisler mean when he says that God *cannot* save all men? I assume Geisler agrees that God has the power to change the disposition of the fallen sinner's will to the end that the sinner would then believe. I am confident that Geisler's "cannot" really means "may not." That is, he sees the Reformed view of regeneration and effectual calling as violating the sinner's free will. Such a violation would not be "right" for God to do. Since the perfect moral character of God restrains him from doing anything wrong, it follows that God "cannot" do what he may not do. In other words, Geisler's *cannot* is shorthand for *will not:* God will not act in such a way that violates the free will of man. This is small consolation to the sinner in hell who would probably be more than willing to have his will violated to get out of that place.

The monergistic regeneration of Reformed theology, however, does not violate the sinner's will. Indeed it is a *change* of the sinner's will wrought by the sovereign agency of God. It is precisely this work of God that liberates the sinner from slavery. It is a strange thing to deem the liberation of an enslaved will as a violation of freedom. It is God's work of freeing, not violating, that is in view.

Throughout this book we have seen the close relationship between one's view of the fall, regeneration, and free will. These matters may be distinguished, but never separated from one another. If the fall renders man morally unable, dead in sin, and enslaved to sin, then human freedom must be viewed in one way. If the fall is not so radical, then the will of man is viewed differently. How we view our fallen condition, then, has radical implications for how we understand both the nature and necessity of regeneration as it relates to faith. This in turn greatly influences how we understand the biblical doctrine of election. From Augustine to the Reformers and Jonathan Edwards, down to the present, those who believe that the fallen sinner retains the capacity to choose what he desires but is enslaved by these desires, rest their confidence in the knowledge that salvation is of the Lord and those whom the Son makes free are free indeed.

Soli Deo gloria.

Notes

Introduction, Evangelicalism and an Ancient Heresy

1. J. I. Packer and O. R. Johnston, "Historical and Theological Introduction," in Martin Luther, *The Bondage of the Will*, trans. J. I. Packer and O. R. Johnston (Cambridge: James Clarke / Westwood, N.J.: Revell, 1957), pp. 57–58. With regard to the contemporary status of "Lutheran orthodoxy," Packer and Johnston cite H. J. Iwand's analysis in a German edition of Luther's *The Bondage of the Will* (Munich, 1954).

2. Ibid., p. 58.

3. Ibid., pp. 58–59.

4. Ibid., p. 59.

5. Ibid., pp. 59–60.

Chapter 1, We Are Capable of Obedience: Pelagius

1. Adolph Harnack, *History of Dogma*, part 2, book 2, trans. James Millar (1898; New York: Dover, 1961), p. 174.

2. Ibid., p. 169.

3. Philip Schaff, *History of the Christian Church*, 8 vols. (1907–10; Grand Rapids: Eerdmans, 1952–53), 3:802–3. Schaff's source is Augustine, *On the Grace of Christ and on Original Sin* (418), responding to Pelagius, *Defense of the Freedom of the Will*.

4. Pelagius, quoted in Harnack, *History of Dogma*, p. 193.

5. Schaff, *History of the Christian Church*, 3:803–4.

6. Ibid., 3:805–6.

7. Pelagius, *Marius Com.*, 2.10. Quoted in Reinhold Seeberg, *Text-Book of the History of Doctrines*, vol. 1, *History of Doctrines in the Ancient Church*, trans. Charles E. Hay (1905; Grand Rapids: Baker, 1977), p. 334.

8. Pelagius, Letter to Demetrius, 8. Quoted in Seeberg, *History of Doctrines*, 1:335.

9. Jaroslav Pelikan, *The Christian Tradition: A History of the Development of Doctrine*, vol. 1, *The Emergence of the Catholic Tradition, 100–600* (Chicago and London: University of Chicago, 1971), p. 314. The three quotations are from the following: (1) Augustine, *On the Proceedings of Pelagius* (417), 22.46; (2) Augustine, *On the Grace of Christ and on Original Sin* (418), 35.38; and (3) Augustine, *Retractations* (426), 2.68.

10. Seeberg, *History of Doctrines*, 1:336. The first quote is from Pelagius, Letter to Demetrius, 8; the second, from Augustine, *On the Grace of Christ*, 7.8.

11. Harnack, *History of Dogma*, p. 175.

12. Seeberg, *History of Doctrines*, 1:354. Both quotes in this paragraph are from Augustine, *On the Proceedings of Pelagius* (417), 19.43, 6.16.

13. Seeberg, *History of Doctrines*, 1:354.

14. Jerome, Letter to Augustine (419). Quoted in Schaff, *History of the Christian Church*, 3:796.

15. Augustine, *On the Proceedings of Pelagius*. Quoted in Schaff, *History of the Christian Church*, 3:796.

16. Pope Innocent, Epistle 31.6. Quoted in Harnack, *History of Dogma*, p. 182.

17. Peter Brown, *Augustine of Hippo: A Biography* (London: Faber and Faber, 1967 / Los Angeles: University of California, 1969), pp. 359–60.

18. Schaff, *History of the Christian Church*, 3:799. In a note Schaff points out that the third of these canons may not be authentic.

19. Seeberg, *History of Doctrines*, 1:356.

20. Schaff, *History of the Christian Church*, 3:815.

Chapter 2, We Are Incapable of Obedience: Augustine

1. Benjamin Breckinridge Warfield, "Augustine," in Warfield, *Studies in Tertullian and Augustine*, ed. Ethelbert D. Warfield et al. (1930; Grand Rapids: Baker, 1981), p. 128. This article was reprinted in Warfield, *Calvin and Augustine*, ed. Samuel G. Craig (Philadelphia: Presbyterian and Reformed, 1956), pp. 305–26 (see p. 320 for this quote). This article originally appeared in James Hastings, ed., *Encyclopedia of Religion and Ethics* (New York: Scribner, 1909), 2:219–24.

2. Warfield, *Studies in Tertullian and Augustine*, p. 130; Warfield, *Calvin and Augustine*, p. 322.

3. Augustine, *The Enchiridion: On Faith, Hope and Love*, trans. J. F. Shaw, in Augustine, *Basic Writings of Saint Augustine*, ed. Whitney J. Oates, 2 vols. (1948; Grand Rapids: Baker, 1980), 1:673 (chaps. 26–27).

4. Augustine, *The City of God*, trans. Marcus Dods et al., in Augustine, *Basic Writings*, 2:255–56 (14.11).

5. Ibid., 2:257–58 (14.13). "... for the evil act [would] never [have] been done" is "... for the evil act had never been done" in Marcus Dods's translation.

6. Ibid., 2:221 (13.14).

7. Philip Schaff, *History of the Christian Church*, 8 vols. (1907–10; Grand Rapids: Eerdmans, 1952–53), 3:825.

8. Ibid., 3:826–27.

9. Augustine, *The City of God*, in Augustine, *Basic Writings*, 2:260 (14.15). For the sake of readability I have broken up an extremely long sentence ("Therefore, because the sin was a despising of the authority of God ... he had forsaken eternal life.") into five sentences.

10. Schaff, *History of the Christian Church*, 3:839.

11. Augustine, *On Grace and Free Will*, trans. Peter Holmes, in Augustine, *Basic Writings*, 1:758 (chap. 31).

12. Schaff, *History of the Christian Church*, 3:820–21.

13. Augustine, *The Enchiridion*, in Augustine, *Basic Writings*, 1:675 (chap. 30).

14. Norman Geisler makes this observation in public lectures.

15. Augustine, *The Enchiridion*, in Augustine, *Basic Writings*, 1:675 (chap. 30).

16. Reinhold Seeberg, *Text-Book of the History of Doctrines*, vol. 1, *History of Doctrines in the Ancient Church*, trans. Charles E. Hay (1905; Grand Rapids: Baker, 1977), p. 344. After the first sentence Seeberg cites Augustine, *On the Grace of Christ and on Original Sin*, chaps. 18–19.

17. Augustine, *The Enchiridion*, in Augustine, *Basic Writings*, 1:677 (chap. 32).

18. Augustine, *On Grace and Free Will*, in Augustine, *Basic Writings*, 1:756 (chap. 29).

19. Ibid., 1:767 (chap. 41).

20. Augustine, *On the Predestination of the Saints*, trans. R. E. Wallis, in Augustine, *Basic Writings*, 1:809 (chap. 34).

21. Pelagius, quoted in Augustine, *Predestination of the Saints*, 1:810–11 (chap. 36).

22. Augustine, *Predestination of the Saints*, 1:812–13 (chap. 38).

Chapter 3, We Are Capable of Cooperating: Semi-Pelagians

1. Reinhold Seeberg, *Text-Book of the History of Doctrines*, vol. 1, *History of Doctrines in the Ancient Church*, trans. Charles E. Hay (1905; Grand Rapids: Baker, 1977), p. 369.

2. Ibid.

3. Ibid.

4. Philip Schaff, *History of the Christian Church*, 8 vols. (1907–10; Grand Rapids: Eerdmans, 1952–53), 3:861.

5. Seeberg, *History of Doctrines*, 1:370. Seeberg cites John Cassian, *Collationum*, 3.12.

6. Adolph Harnack, *History of Dogma*, part 2, book 2, trans. James Millar (1898; New York: Dover, 1961), p. 247.

7. Seeberg, *History of Doctrines*, 1:371–72.

8. Schaff, *History of the Christian Church*, 3:861.

9. John Cassian, *Collationum*, 13.8, 7. Quoted in Seeberg, *History of Doctrines*, 1:371.

10. Schaff, *History of the Christian Church*, 3:867, 869.

11. *Canons and Decrees of the Council of Trent: Original Text with English Translation*, trans. H. J. Schroeder (London: Herder, 1941), pp. 42–43.

12. Martin Chemnitz, *Examination of the Council of Trent*, trans. Fred Kramer, 4 vols. (St. Louis and London: Concordia, 1971–86), 1:428 (7.2.1). Chemnitz quotes Jacob Payva Andrada, *Orthodox Explanations of the Controverted Points of Religion* (1564).

13. Chemnitz, *Examination of the Council of Trent*, 1:428–29 (7.2.1).

14. *Canons and Decrees of the Council of Trent*, p. 43.

15. John Calvin, *Acts of the Council of Trent: With the Antidote*, ed. and trans. Henry Beveridge (1851), in John Calvin, *Selected Works of John Calvin: Tracts and Letters*, ed. Henry Beveridge and Jules Bonnet, 7 vols. (Grand Rapids: Baker, 1983), 3:147–48. Calvin cites Augustine, *On Rebuke and Grace*, 100.14.

16. Calvin, *Acts of the Council of Trent*, 3:148. The first quote from Augustine is from a letter to Anastas; the second quote is from a sermon on John; the third is unspecified.

17. Quoted in Seeberg, *History of Doctrines*, 2:450.

18. Ibid., 2:451–52.

19. Ibid., 2:452.

20. Harold J. Grimm, *The Reformation Era: 1500–1650* (New York: Macmillan / London: Collier-Macmillan, 1954), p. 533.

21. Seeberg, *History of Doctrines*, 2:455.

22. *Catechism of the Catholic Church* (New York: Pauline, 1994), p. 430 (pars. 1731–32).

23. Ibid., p. 430 (par. 1730). The *Catechism* quotes Vatican II, *Gaudium et spes* (1965), 17. *Gaudium et spes* quotes Ecclesiasticus 15:14.

24. *Catechism of the Catholic Church*, p. 103 (par. 406).

25. Ibid., p. 103.

26. Vatican II, *Gaudium et spes*, 37.2. Quoted in *Catechism of the Catholic Church*, p. 103 (par. 409).

Chapter 4, We Are in Bondage to Sin: Martin Luther

1. Martin Luther, Letter to W. F. Capito, 9 July 1537. Cited in J. I. Packer and O. R. Johnston, "Historical and Theological Introduction," in Martin Luther, *The Bondage of the Will*, trans. J. I. Packer and O. R. Johnston (Cambridge: James Clarke / Westwood, N.J.: Revell, 1957), p. 40.

2. Benjamin Breckinridge Warfield, "The Theology of the Reformation," in Warfield, *Studies in Theology*, ed. Ethelbert D. Warfield et al. (1932; Grand Rapids: Baker, 1981), p. 471. This article originally appeared in *Biblical Review* 2 (1917): 490–512.

3. *"Luthers Schrift* De servo arbitrio *ist das schönste und traftigste Soli Deo gloria, das von der ganzen Reformation gesungen worden ist."* Sigurd Normann, "De servo arbitrio als Ausdruct lutherischen Christentums," *Zeitschrift für systematische Theologie* 14 (1937):338. Translated by Gordon Rupp and quoted in his *The Righteousness of God: Luther Studies: The Birkbeck Lectures in Ecclesiastical History Delivered in the University of Cambridge, 1947* (New York: Philosophical Library, 1953), p. 283. Rupp writes: "But I hope it can be seen why this treatise [Luther's *The Bondage of the Will*] still lives and why it is, as Bishop Normann has it, 'the finest and most powerful Soli Deo Gloria to be sung in the whole period of the Reformation.' " Rupp's translation of Normann is quoted in Packer and Johnston, "Historical and Theological Introduction," p. 41.

4. Erasmus, *Diatribe Concerning Free Will*. Quoted in Martin Luther, *The Bondage of the Will*, p. 74 (2.3).

5. Ibid., p. 76 (2.3).

6. Ibid., p. 78 (2.3).

7. Ibid., pp. 80–81 (2.4).

8. Ibid., p. 81 (2.4).

9. Ibid., pp. 83–84 (2.5).

10. Erasmus, *Diatribe Concerning Free Will*, preface. Quoted in Luther, *The Bondage of the Will*, p. 97 (2.7).

11. Luther, *The Bondage of the Will*, p. 99 (2.7).

12. Ibid., pp. 102–3 (2.8).

13. Ibid., p. 104 (2.9).

14. Ibid., p. 105 (2.9).

15. Ibid., p. 106 (2.9).

16. Erasmus, *Diatribe Concerning Free Will*. Quoted in Luther, *The Bondage of the Will*, p. 137 (4.1).

17. Luther, *The Bondage of the Will*, pp. 138–39 (4.1).

18. Ibid., pp. 144–45 (4.3).

19. Ibid., p. 145 (4.3).

20. Ibid.

21. Erasmus, *Diatribe Concerning Free Will*. Quoted in Luther, *The Bondage of the Will*, p. 145 (4.3).

22. Luther, *The Bondage of the Will*, p. 146 (4.3).

23. Ibid., p. 148 (4.3).

24. Erasmus, *Diatribe Concerning Free Will*. Quoted in Luther, *The Bondage of the Will*, pp. 151–52 (4.5).

25. Luther, *The Bondage of the Will*, p. 153 (4.5).

26. Erasmus, *Diatribe Concerning Free Will*. Quoted in Luther, *The Bondage of the Will*, p. 171 (4.11).

27. Luther, *The Bondage of the Will*, pp. 171–72 (4.11).

28. Ibid., p. 174 (4.11).

29. Erasmus, *Diatribe Concerning Free Will*. Quoted in Luther, *The Bondage of the Will*, p. 187 (4.16).

30. Luther, *The Bondage of the Will*, p. 187 (4.16).

31. Ibid., p. 207 (5.6).

32. Erasmus, *Diatribe Concerning Free Will*. Quoted in Luther, *The Bondage of the Will*, p. 220 (5.10).

33. Luther, *The Bondage of the Will*, p. 220 (5.10).

34. Ibid., p. 260 (5.7).

35. Ibid., p. 261 (5.7).

36. Ibid., p. 262 (5.7).

Chapter 5, We Are Voluntary Slaves: John Calvin

1. John Calvin, *Institutes of the Christian Religion*, 2 vols., trans. Henry Beveridge (1845; Grand Rapids: Eerdmans, 1964), 1:223 (2.2.1).

2. Ibid.

3. Ibid., 1:225 (2.2.3). Cicero, *Nature of the Gods*, 3.36.86–87.

4. Calvin, *Institutes of the Christian Religion*, 1:225 (2.2.4).

5. Ibid., 1:225–26 (2.2.4). Chrysostom, *De proditione Judaeorum*, 1; and *Homilies on Genesis*, 19.1. Jerome, *Dialogus contra Pelagianos*, 3.1.

6. Calvin, *Institutes of the Christian Religion*, 1:226 (2.2.4).

7. Ibid., 1:227–28 (2.2.5). See Peter Lombard, *Sentences*, 2.25.9.

8. Calvin, *Institutes of the Christian Religion*, 1:229–30 (2.2.7–8).

9. Ibid., 1:232 (2.2.11). Augustine, *Letters*, 113.3.22.

10. Calvin, *Institutes of the Christian Religion*, 1:236 (2.2.15).

11. Ibid., 1:238 (2.2.18).

12. Ibid., 1:249 (2.3.1).

13. Ibid., 1:253 (2.3.5).

14. Ibid., 1:254 (2.3.5).

15. Ibid., 1:255 (2.3.6).

16. Chrysostom, *De ferendis reprehensionibus*, 6; *Homilies on the Gospel of John*, 10.1. Quoted in Calvin, *Institutes of the Christian Religion*, 1:260 (2.3.10).

17. Calvin, *Institutes of the Christian Religion*, 1:260 (2.3.10).

18. Ibid., 1:263–64 (2.3.13). See Augustine, *On Rebuke and Grace to Valentinus*, 14.45.

19. John Calvin, *Articles Agreed upon by the Faculty of Sacred Theology of Paris, in Reference to Matters of Faith at Present Controverted; with the Antidote*, ed. and trans. Henry Beveridge (1844), in John Calvin, *Selected Works of John Calvin: Tracts and Letters*, ed. Henry Beveridge and Jules Bonnet, 7 vols. (Grand Rapids: Baker, 1983), 1:75.

20. Ibid., 1:76. The first reference to Augustine is to his *Letter to Boniface*, 3; the second, to his *Homil. in Joan.*, 53.

21. Ibid., 1:76–77.

22. John Calvin, *Commentary on the Gospel According to John*, trans. William Pringle, 2 vols. (1847–48; Grand Rapids: Baker, 1979), 1:257 (on John 6:44).

23. Ibid.

24. Ibid., 1:276 (on John 6:65).

25. John Calvin, *The Epistles of Paul the Apostle to the Galatians, Ephesians, Philippians and Colossians*, trans. T. H. L. Parker, Calvin's Commentaries, ed. David W. Torrance and Thomas F. Torrance (Edinburgh: Oliver and Boyd / Grand Rapids: Eerdmans, 1965), p. 139 (on Eph. 2:1).

26. Ibid., p. 141 (on Eph. 2:3).

27. Ibid., p. 142 (on Eph. 2:4).

28. Ibid., p. 144. The translator, T. H. L. Parker, says of his decision to translate *opus* as "work": "*Opus* can mean 'workmanship' (as AV) and this would be the smoother rendering here. But I have preferred 'work' to preserve the link with Calvin's characteristic concept of the *opus dei* [the work of God]."

29. Ibid., p. 145 (on Eph. 2:10).

30. Ibid., pp. 145–46 (on Eph. 2:10).

31. John Calvin, *The Epistles of Paul the Apostle to the Romans and to the Thessalonians*, trans. Ross MacKenzie, Calvin's Commentaries, ed. David W. Torrance and Thomas F. Torrance (Edinburgh: Oliver and Boyd / Grand Rapids: Eerdmans, 1960), p. 205 (on Rom. 9:16).

32. Ibid., pp. 205–6 (on Rom. 9:16).

33. Francis Turretin, *Institutes of Elenctic Theology*, 3 vols., trans. George Musgrave Giger, ed. James T. Dennison Jr. (Phillipsburg, N.J.: P & R, 1992–97), 2:542 (15.5.1).

34. Ibid., 2:543 (15.5.4).

35. Turretin, *Institutes of Elenctic Theology*, 2:543 (15.5.6). See *Canons and Decrees of the Council of Trent: Original Text with English Translation*, trans. H. J. Schroeder (London and St. Louis: Herder, 1941), pp. 42–43, where this article is translated as follows: "If anyone says that man's free will moved and aroused by God, by assenting to God's call and action, in no way cooperates toward disposing and preparing itself to obtain the grace of justification, that it cannot refuse its assent if it wishes, but that, as something inanimate, it does nothing whatever and is merely passive, let him be anathema."

36. Turretin, *Institutes of Elenctic Theology*, 2:543 (15.5.7).

37. Ibid., 2:544 (15.5.7).

38. Ibid., 2:546 (15.6).

39. Ibid., 2:546 (15.6.1).

40. Ibid., 2:547 (15.6.2).

41. Ibid., 2:552 (15.6.16).

Chapter 6, We Are Free to Believe: James Arminius

1. James Arminius, *The Public Disputations of James Arminius, D.D.*, in James Arminius, *The Works of James Arminius: The London Edition*, trans. James and William Nichols, 3 vols. (1825–75; Grand Rapids: Baker, 1986), 2:192 (11.7). Disputation 11 is titled "On the Free Will of Man and Its Powers."

2. Ibid.

3. Ibid., 2:192–93 (11.8).

4. Ibid., 2:193 (11.9).

5. Ibid., 2:193–94 (11.10–11).

6. Ibid., 2:194–95 (11.12).

7. Ibid., 2:195 (11.13).

8. Ibid., 2:196 (11). The first paragraph is a quotation of Augustine, *Against Two Letters of the Pelagians;* the second paragraph, of Bernardus, *On Free Will and Grace.*

9. James Arminius, *Certain Articles to Be Diligently Examined and Weighed: Because Some Controversy Has Arisen Concerning Them among Even Those Who Profess the*

Reformed Religion, in Arminius, *The Works of James Arminius: The London Edition,* 2:721 (17.4). Article 17 is titled "On the Vocation of Sinners to Communion with Christ, and to a Participation of His Benefits."

10. Ibid., 2:721 (17.5).

11. Ibid., 2:721–22 (17.12).

12. Ibid., 2:722 (17.13).

13. Ibid., 2:722 (17.16).

14. Ibid., 2:722 (17.17).

15. Frances Turretin, *Institutes of Elenctic Theology,* 3 vols., trans. George Musgrave Giger, ed. James T. Dennison Jr. (Phillipsburg, N.J.: P & R, 1992–97), 2:547–48 (15.6.6–7).

16. James Arminius, *The Apology or Defence of James Arminius, D.D., against Thirty-one Theological Articles,* in Arminius, *The Works of James Arminius: The London Edition,* 2:52 (against article 27).

17. Philip Schaff, *History of the Christian Church,* 8 vols. (1907–10; Grand Rapids: Eerdmans, 1952–53), 8:280.

18. Williston Walker, *A History of the Christian Church,* rev. Cyril C. Richardson, Wilhelm Pauck, and Robert T. Handy (New York: Scribner's, 1959), p. 399.

19. Ibid., p. 400.

20. Roger Nicole, "Arminianism," in Everett F. Harrison, ed., *Baker's Dictionary of Theology* (Grand Rapids: Baker, 1960), p. 64.

21. *The Remonstrance of 1610,* appendix C in Peter Y. De Jong, ed., *Crisis in the Reformed Churches: Essays in Commemoration of the Great Synod of Dort, 1618–1619* (Grand Rapids: Reformed Fellowship, 1968), pp. 208–9. The Scripture reference is rendered incorrectly by De Jong as John 13:5. See also Philip Schaff, ed., *The Creeds of Christendom: With a History and Critical Notes,* rev. David S. Schaff, 3 vols., 6th ed. (1931; Grand Rapids: Baker, 1990), 3:546–47.

22. *The Counter Remonstrance of 1611,* appendix D in De Jong, ed., *Crisis in the Reformed Churches,* pp. 211–12.

23. *The Opinions of the Remonstrants,* trans. Anthony A. Hoekema, appendix H in De Jong, ed., *Crisis in the Reformed Churches,* p. 226.

24. *The Canons of Dort,* appendix I in De Jong, ed., *Crisis in the Reformed Churches,* pp. 246–47. Article 10 of the third and fourth heads of doctrine ("The Corruption of Man, His Conversion to God, and the Manner Thereof"). See also Schaff, ed., *The Creeds of Christendom,* 3:589–90.

25. *The Canons of Dort,* in De Jong, ed., *Crisis in the Reformed Churches,* p. 247. Articles 11 and 12 of the third and fourth heads of doctrine. See also Schaff, ed., *The Creeds of Christendom,* 3:590.

26. *The Canons of Dort,* in De Jong, ed., *Crisis in the Reformed Churches,* pp. 249, 251–52. Paragraphs 6–8 of "Rejection of Errors," the third and fourth heads of doctrine.

27. Clark H. Pinnock, "From Augustine to Arminius: A Pilgrimage in Theology," in Clark H. Pinnock, ed., *The Grace of God, the Will of Man: A Case for Arminianism* (Grand Rapids: Academie / Zondervan, 1988), p. 15.

28. Ibid.

29. Ibid., p. 27.

30. Ibid.

31. Ibid., p. 26.

32. Ibid., p. 25.

33. William Lane Craig, "Middle Knowledge: A Calvinist-Arminian Rapprochement?" in Pinnock, ed., *The Grace of God,* pp. 141–64.

34. Pinnock, ed., *The Grace of God,* pp. 25–26.

35. Clark H. Pinnock, Richard Rice, John Sanders, William Hasker, and David Basinger, *The Openness of God: A Biblical Challenge to the Traditional Understanding of God* (Downers Grove, Ill.: InterVarsity / Carlisle, Cumb.: Paternoster, 1994), p. 9.

Chapter 7, We Are Inclined to Sin: Jonathan Edwards

1. Jonathan Edwards, *The Great Christian Doctrine of Original Sin Defended: Evidences of Its Truth Produced, and Arguments to the Contrary Answered,* in Jonathan Edwards, *The Works of Jonathan Edwards, A.M.,* 10th ed., 2 vols. (1865; Edinburgh / Carlisle, Penn.: Banner of Truth, 1979), 1:145. The author's preface is dated 1757.

2. Ibid., 1:151, col. a.

3. Ibid.

4. Ibid.

5. Ibid., 1:152, col. a.

6. Ibid., 1:152, col. b.

7. Ibid., 1:156, col. b.

8. Ibid., 1:173, col. a.

9. Ibid., 1:197, col. b.

10. Ibid., 1:210, col. b.

11. Ibid., 1:214, col. a.

12. Paul Ramsey, "Editor's Introduction," in Jonathan Edwards, *Freedom of the Will,* ed. Paul Ramsey, The Works of Jonathan Edwards, ed. Perry Miller, vol. 1 (New Haven and London: Yale University, 1957), pp. 1–2. The full title of Edwards's work was originally *A Careful and Strict Enquiry into the Modern Prevailing Notions of That Freedom of Will, Which Is Supposed to Be Essential to Moral Agency, Virtue and Vice, Reward and Punishment, Praise and Blame.* Ramsey alludes to David F. Swenson, translator of Søren Kierkegaard's *Philosophical Fragments* (1936), *Concluding Unscientific Postscript* (1941), *Three Discourses on Imagined Occasions* (1941), volume 1 of *Either/Or* (1941), and *Works of Love* (1946); and author of *Something about Kierkegaard* (Minneapolis: Augsburg, 1941).

13. Edwards, *Freedom of the Will,* p. 133.

14. Ibid., p. 137.

15. Ibid.

16. Ibid., p. 139. Quotes from John Locke, *An Essay Concerning Human Understanding,* 7th ed. (1716), 2.21.30.

17. Edwards, *Freedom of the Will,* p. 141.

18. Ibid.

19. John H. Gerstner, "Augustine, Luther, Calvin, and Edwards on the Bondage of the Will," in Thomas R. Schreiner and Bruce A. Ware, eds., *The Grace of God, the Bondage of the Will,* 2 vols. (Grand Rapids: Baker, 1995), 2:291. Quotation from John Preston, "Sermon on Hebrews 5:12," in John Preston, *Works,* 2:158.

20. Edwards, *Freedom of the Will,* p. 142.

21. Ibid.

22. Ibid., p. 149.

23. Ibid., p. 152.

24. Ibid., p. 153.

25. Ibid., p. 155.

26. See R. C. Sproul, *Not a Chance: The Myth of Chance in Modern Science and Cosmology* (Grand Rapids: Baker, 1994).

27. Edwards, *Freedom of the Will,* p. 159.

28. Ibid., p. 164.
29. Ibid., pp. 164–65.
30. Ibid., pp. 172–73.
31. Ibid., p. 184.
32. Ibid., p. 197.

Chapter 8, We Are Not Depraved by Nature: Charles Grandison Finney

1. Charles G. Finney, *Finney's Systematic Theology*, 3d ed., ed. Dennis Carroll, Bill Nicely, and L. G. Parkhurst Jr. (1878; Minneapolis: Bethany, 1994).

2. Charles White, "Review of Keith J. Hardman, *Charles Grandison Finney, 1792–1875*," *Fides et Historia* 21 (January 1989): 89.

3. Keith J. Hardman, *Charles Grandison Finney, 1792–1875: Revivalist and Reformer* (Syracuse: Syracuse University, 1987; Grand Rapids: Baker, 1990), p. xii.

4. Robert Godfrey, "Cambridge Highlights," *Modern Reformation* 5 (July 1996), p. 7.

5. Ibid. See Robert Godfrey, "The Reformation of Worship," in James Montgomery Boice and Benjamin E. Sasse, eds., *Here We Stand! A Call from Confessing Evangelicals* (Grand Rapids: Baker, 1996), pp. 157–72. Godfrey quotes Benjamin Breckinridge Warfield, "The Theology of Charles G. Finney," in Warfield, *Perfectionism*, ed. Ethelbert D. Warfield et al., 2 vols. (1931–32; Grand Rapids: Baker, 1981), 2:193. Warfield's article was reprinted in Warfield, *Perfectionism*, ed. Samuel G. Craig (Philadelphia: Presbyterian and Reformed, 1958), pp. 166–215 (see p. 193 for this quote). Warfield's article originally appeared in *The Princeton Theological Review* 19 (1921): 568–619.

6. L. G. Parkhurst Jr., "Finney's Theology," in Finney, *Finney's Systematic Theology*, p. xxii.

7. Parkhurst, "Finney's Theology," p. xviii. In a note Parkhurst singles out as an example Keith J. Hardman. Ibid., p. xxv (n. 17).

8. Finney, *Systematic Theology*, pp. 360–61 (lecture 25, "Justification").
9. Ibid., p. 361 (lect. 25).
10. Ibid., p. 362 (lect. 25).
11. Ibid., p. 219 (lecture 13, "Atonement").
12. Ibid.
13. Ibid., p. 212 (lect. 13).
14. Ibid., p. 214 (lect. 13).
15. Ibid., p. 213 (lect. 13).
16. Ibid., p. 223 (lecture 14, "Extent of Atonement").
17. Ibid., p. 366 (lecture 25, "Justification").
18. Ibid., pp. 368–69 (lect. 25).
19. Ibid., p. 369 (lect. 25).
20. Ibid., pp. 370–72 (lect. 25).
21. Ibid., p. 377 (lect. 25).
22. Ibid., p. 243 (lecture 16, "Moral Depravity").
23. Ibid., p. 245 (lect. 16).
24. Ibid., p. 250 (lect. 16).
25. Ibid.
26. Ibid., p. 262 (lect. 16).
27. Ibid., p. 267 (lect. 16).
28. Ibid., p. 307 (lecture 20, "Natural Ability").
29. Ibid., p. 305 (lect. 20).
30. Ibid., p. 307 (lect. 20).

31. Ibid., p. 269 (lecture 17, "Regeneration").
32. Ibid., p. 276 (lect. 17).
33. Ibid., p. 274 (lect. 17).

Chapter 9, We Are Able to Believe: Lewis Sperry Chafer

1. John H. Gerstner, *Wrongly Dividing the Word of Truth: A Critique of Dispensationalism* (Brentwood, Tenn.: Wolgemuth & Hyatt, 1991). Chapter 7 (pp. 105–46) is titled "Spurious Calvinism."

2. Lewis Sperry Chafer, *Systematic Theology,* 8 vols. (1947–48; Grand Rapids: Kregel, 1993), 2:285.

3. Ibid., 2:283.

4. Ibid.

5. Ibid., 2:286–87. See W. G. T. Shedd, *Dogmatic Theology,* 3 vols. (1888–94; Nashville: Nelson, 1980), 2:196–200.

6. Chafer, *Systematic Theology,* 1:238–39.

7. Ibid., 1:240.

8. Ibid., 1:241.

9. Ibid., 1:243. Quotes from John Dick, *Lectures on Theology,* 2 vols. (Philadelphia: Greenough, 1839), 1:357–58.

10. Ibid., 6:113.

11. Ibid., 7:265.

12. Ibid., 6:117–18. Quotes from John F. Walvoord, *The Doctrine of the Holy Spirit: A Study in Pneumatology* (Dallas: Dallas Theological Seminary, 1943), pp. 145ff.

13. Ibid., 3:335.

14. Gerstner, *Wrongly Dividing the Word of Truth,* p. 109.

15. Chafer, *Systematic Theology,* 6:106–7.

16. Ibid., 6:109.

17. Ibid., 6:117. Quotes from Walvoord, *The Doctrine of the Holy Spirit,* pp. 144–45.

18. R. C. Sproul, "A Serious Charge," in Michael Horton, ed., *The Agony of Deceit* (Chicago: Moody, 1990), pp. 44–45.

19. Gerstner, *Wrongly Dividing the Word of Truth,* p. 147.

20. Ibid., p. 145. See J. F. Strombeck, *Disciplined by Grace* (Chicago: Moody, 1946), p. 137.

21. Chafer, *Systematic Theology,* 7:136.

22. Gerstner, *Wrongly Dividing the Word of Truth,* p. 137. Quotes Billy Graham, *How to Be Born Again* (Waco, Tex.: Word, 1977), pp. 150, 152, 157. Italics in the first quote are Gerstner's.

23. Gerstner, *Wrongly Dividing the Word of Truth,* p. 138. Quotes Billy Graham, *How to Be Born Again,* p. 168; and Lewis Sperry Chafer and John Walvoord, *Major Bible Themes,* 2d ed. (Grand Rapids: Zondervan, 1974), p. 99 (italics are Gerstner's).

24. Chafer, *Systematic Theology,* 1:229–30.

25. Ibid., 1:230.

26. Ibid., 1:231.

27. Gerstner, *Wrongly Dividing the Word of Truth,* pp. 111. Quotes C. I. Scofield, ed., *Scofield Reference Bible* (New York: Oxford University, 1909), p. 1311.

28. Gerstner, *Wrongly Dividing the Word of Truth,* pp. 111–12.

29. Ibid., p. 115. Quotes Norman L. Geisler, "God, Evil and Dispensations," in Donald K. Campbell, ed., *Walvoord: A Tribute* (Chicago: Moody, 1982), p. 102.

Latin Glossary

adjutorium ([place of] help, assistance), 52, 57

amentes (mad), 127

anima (soul), 127

a priori (from the former; deductively), 36

articuli Arminiani sive remonstrantia (Arminian articles or remonstrance), 135

attenuatem (weakened), 125

bonum naturae (good of nature), 35

captivatum (imprisoned), 125

collationes patrum (comparative examinations of the Fathers), 71

concupiscentia (sin, evil), 58, 61

constituti (placed), 127

contingit (granted), 130

cooperans (working together), 74

cor ecclesiae (heart of the church), 22, 87

de libero arbitrio (on the freedom of the will), 43

de natura (on nature), 43

de servo arbitrio (on the bondage of the will), 21, 87

diatribe seu collatio de libero arbitrio (discourse or comparative examination regarding free will), 87

enchiridion (handbook, manual), 51, 54, 63, 65

ens perfictisimus (most perfect being), 89

ex nihilo (out of nothing), 165

fides viva (vital, living faith), 180

gratia praeveniens (prevenient grace), 74

habitus (state, condition, habit), 60

ingeneratae (produced), 128

infirmitas liberi arbitrii (infirm free will), 72

illuminatio et doctrina (illumination and doctrine), 40

impotentia (weakness), 127

in equilibrio (in balance, equal weight), 163

libero arbitrio semper co-operatur (free will always works together with [cooperates]), 72

libertas (liberty), 63, 65

liberum arbitrium (free will), 36, 63, 65

libido (desire), 64

massa peccati (mass of sin), 51

mundus (world), 17

necessitatem infallibilem (necessity of infallibility), 102

necessitatem violentam (necessity of force), 102

non posse non more (inability not to die), 54

non posse non peccare (inability not to sin), 182

non posse peccare (inability to sin), 52–53

operans (working, operating), 74

ordo salutis (order of salvation), 23, 193

peccatum originis (original sin), 38
perficere (complete), 126
posse mori (ability to die), 54, 58
posse non mori (ability not to die), 54, 58
posse non peccare (ability not to sin), 52
posse peccare (ability to sin), 52, 56
possibilitas boni et mali (equal ability to do good or evil), 36
possibilitas utriusque partis (possibility of either side [part]), 65
potens (capable), 128

reatus (guilt), 61
reductio ad absurdum (reduction to the absurd), 96

saeculum (world), 17
sensu (feeling, sense), 132

sicut erat dei (you shall be as gods), 18
simul iustus et peccator (at the same time just and sinner), 178
sine qua non (without which, not; something that is indispensable), 35, 51, 178, 179, 200
sola (alone, only), 88, 122
sola fide (faith alone), 21, 24, 25, 26, 122, 148, 172, 174, 177, 179, 180
sola gratia (grace alone), 24, 26, 74, 87, 122, 139, 148, 185
soli Deo gloria (glory to God alone), 204

tabula rasa (blank tablet), 36
tantum capere (capable), 129
tradux peccati (transmitted sin), 38

venio (to come), 129

Index of Personal Names

Index of Scripture

R. C. Sproul is the author of *Faith Alone: The Evangelical Doctrine of Justification. Willing to Believe: The Controversy over Free Will* is a sequel to *Faith Alone,* dealing with the evangelical doctrines of man's total depravity and God's irresistible grace in salvation.

Sproul has written approximately forty books. In addition to many volumes on theology, apologetics, and ethics, he has written a novel, a biography, and two children's books. He has also edited several volumes, including a festschrift for John H. Gerstner, a seminary textbook, and the *New Geneva Study Bible.* (See page 2 for a partial list of Sproul's publications.)

Sproul founded Ligonier Ministries in 1971, a teaching ministry to assist the church in nurturing believers and equipping them for the ministries to which God has called them. Ligonier sponsors a radio program, "Renewing Your Mind," which features Sproul and is broadcast nationally, five days a week. Sproul has taught theology to hundreds of thousands of people through books, radio, audiotapes, videotapes, seminars, sermons, seminary classes, and other forums.

Ligonier Ministries sponsors several seminars each year, the largest one in Orlando every winter. Ligonier publishes a monthly periodical, *Tabletalk,* and has its own web site (see page 4 for the address).

Sproul is professor of systematic theology and apologetics at Knox Theological Seminary in Fort Lauderdale. He earned a B.A. degree from Westminster College, a B.D. from Pittsburgh Theological Seminary, and a Drs. from the Free University of Amsterdam. He is ordained in the Presbyterian Church in America.

In 1994 *Christianity Today* asked a select list of "critics," "What theologian or biblical scholar has most shaped your Christian life?" Third on the list (and the only American in the top four) was R. C. Sproul.